TALES FROM THE
NEW YORK GIANTS
SIDELINE

TALES FROM THE
NEW YORK GIANTS
SIDELINE

A COLLECTION OF THE GREATEST
GIANTS STORIES EVER TOLD

PAUL SCHWARTZ
FOREWORDS BY WELLINGTON MARA
AND JOHN MARA

SPORTS
PUBLISHING

Sports Publishing books may be purchased in bulk at special discounts for
sales promotion, corporate gifts, fund-raising, or educational purposes.
Special editions can also be created to specifications. For details, contact the
Special Sales Department, Sports Publishing, 307 West 36th Street, 11th
Floor, New York, NY 10018 or sportspubbooks@skyhorsepublishing.com.

Sports Publishing® is a registered trademark of Skyhorse Publishing, Inc.®,
a Delaware corporation.

Visit our website at www.sportspubbooks.com.

10 9 8 7 6 5 4 3 2 1

Library of Congress Cataloging-in-Publication Data is available on file.

Cover design by Tom Lau
Cover photo: AP Images

ISBN: 978-1-68358-162-8
Ebook ISBN: 978-1-68358-168-0

Printed in the United States of America

CONTENTS

FOREWORD

BY WELLINGTON MARA

The 2004 season is the 80th in New York Giants history. The franchise has played more than 1,100 games, including postseason contests, among them some of the greatest and most memorable games in NFL history. Every Giants fan is familiar with the Super Bowl victories, the championship game triumphs, the big wins over our division rivals—and, of course, the disappointment of the 1958 championship game against Baltimore, a game some like to call the "Greatest Game Ever Played."

But to me, the history of the Giants is written not so much in the games we play, but in the people who play them. Our players, coaches, and front office people have given the organization its character and personality and made this a great franchise.

Every one of them has a story to tell, from Frank Gifford and Sam Huff—two of the 27 members of the Pro Football Hall of Fame with a Giants connection—to Phil Simms, Tiki Barber, and Ernie Accorsi. It is with them we share the joy of our greatest successes and the hurt from our seasons of disappointment. They provide the details of the day-to-day life away from the spotlight, the countless meetings and practices and the relationships and bonds that become the backbone of the organization.

Our franchise has a special bond with its fans, and it has survived many ups and downs. That is reflected with great care and in great detail by Paul Schwartz in *Tales from the New York Giants Sideline*.

From Y.A. Tittle to Simms, from Ron Johnson to Barber, the men who were and are Giants share many of the best stories ever

(Photo courtesy of the New York Giants)

told about our franchise. This book will take you from the locker room to the sideline, from the searing heat of training camp practices to the numbing cold of a January postseason game. It will take you through some difficult seasons as well as through Super Bowl championships.

Whether the stories relate to our seasons of disappointment or our years of triumph, you will see that we maintained our sense of humor. And we retained our sense of community. These reflections will shed light on those seasons for even our most ardent and loyal supporters.

Many of the most legendary figures in franchise history shared their thoughts. When Sam Huff and Dick Lynch talk about their Giants careers, the 1960s suddenly seem like they were yesterday. Bob Tucker and Billy Taylor recall the difficult years of the 1970s. Bill Parcells and Mark Collins remember the 1986 and 1990 championship seasons, while Glenn Parker and Brad Daluiso bring to life the 2000 season, when the Giants won the NFC Championship and played in Super Bowl XXXV.

Members of the Giants family warmly remember George Young, and the brilliance and humor he brought to his job as general manager for 19 years. Entertaining stories about coaches like Alex Webster and Parcells permeate both our history and the book. And, of course, almost everyone has a Lawrence Taylor story or memory to share.

The long history of the Giants has been affectionately and captivatingly recalled here by the men who made it.

(Editor's note: Wellington Mara passed away on October 25, 2005, at the age of 89.)

FOREWORD

BY JOHN MARA

Much has happened with our franchise since *Tales from the New York Giants Sideline* was originally published in 2004.

We lost the organization's patriarch and matriarch, my father and mother, in 2005 and 2015, respectively. Bob Tisch, a wonderful partner, also passed away in 2005.

Along with Steve Tisch, I have strived to uphold the principles established for our company. As my father would often say, "Once a Giant, always a Giant." It really is all about the people who have written the history and laid the foundation for the tradition of the New York Giants.

Once again, Paul Schwartz provides insight and color from those personalities in this updated version of his book. Tom Coughlin is now a two-time Super Bowl-winning head coach. Eli Manning is a two-time Super Bowl MVP, thanks in no small part to his miraculous scramble and throw to David Tyree in Super Bowl XLII as well as his laser to Mario Manningham along the sideline to start the game-winning drive in Super Bowl XLVI.

And, in 2016, Ben McAdoo became the 17th head coach in our team's history.

But as any fan of the Giants knows, our history features more than the Parcells, Simms, Taylors, Tittles, Giffords, Coughlins, Mannings, and McAdoos. It is also in great part about the Tyrees, the Manninghams, the Blackburns, and the lesser-known players who stepped up and contributed in the most crucial moments.

We continue to write our history, but we hope you enjoy these stories and their authors from our first 92 seasons.

John Mara is the president and chief executive officer of the New York Giants.

ACKNOWLEDGMENTS

During the process of writing a book such as this, it is impossible not to receive an education about the players, coaches, fans, games, scores, impossible triumphs, and devastating failures contained in the long and storied history of the New York Giants. Along the way, one revealed truth rose above all others: The Giants matter to so many people.

Interviews with Giants players spanning a variety of decades revealed a few constant themes. Some were big winners, even champions; others were consistent losers. Some were transcendent stars; others were the grunts who made up the bulk of a roster. The pervading attitude, though, was one of pride in having worn the Giants uniform, appreciation for the loyalty of the fans, and gratitude for having played for an owner such as Wellington Mara.

Indeed, the Mara family is the lifeblood that courses through the franchise. Prior to a lengthy interview, Wellington Mara warned me "I'm not a self-starter," but when prodded just a bit, he recalled—in affectionate terms—so many details of his 80 years in the game. His oldest son, John, the heir to Wellington's Giants throne, initially expressed dismay that he had little to offer. His concern was unwarranted, as these pages will attest.

Wellington Mara passed away in 2005 at the age of 89. In their first game after their patriarch's death, the Giants—mourning, motivated, and wearing "WTM" patches on the chest of their blue home uniforms—defeated the Redskins 36-0. John Mara, along with co-owner Steve Tisch, carries on Wellington Mara's legacy to this day.

A note of appreciation also goes to Pat Hanlon, the Giants' senior vice president of communications, and Peter John-Baptiste, the Giants former director of public relations, who were helpful in facilitating several conversations with former Giants players and coaches.

In the years since this book was first published, the Giants added two more Super Bowl trophies, saw Eli Manning evolve from an unsure young quarterback into a champion, and ushered in the arrival of megastar Odell Beckham Jr. and unassuming head coach Ben McAdoo. As always, in good times and bad, the Giants continue to matter.

My wonderful wife, Jutta, always offered her support, and my extraordinary children, Elena and Jared, were seven and five, respectively, when this book was first published and at that time were constantly interested in how many pages I had left. Elena, 20, and Jared, 18, are nearly the ages of many of the players chronicled here and are even more extraordinary now than they were then.

Finally, *Tales from the New York Giants Sideline* is dedicated to the memory of my beloved mother, Elaine Schwartz, who didn't love football but would have cherished this book as much as my devoted father, Jack, already does.

Chapter 1

TRAINING CAMP

Nose for the Ball

At 17 years old, Wellington Mara in 1933 attended his first Giants training camp, when the team was stationed in Pompton Lakes, New Jersey. He did not escape unscathed.

Already a co-owner along with his older brother Jack, Mara liked to find ways to help out on the field. He learned soon enough that the sideline was a safer place to be.

"Mel Hein gave me my first football injury," Mara said.

On his way to a Hall of Fame career, Hein was a remarkable iron man, a center who never missed a game in his 15 years in the NFL. Hein, one of the Giants' true stars—he was the league's Most Valuable Player in 1938—nearly gained recognition for the wrong reason.

"They were punting, Hein was snapping the ball back, really it was a warm-up," Mara said. "I was retrieving the balls, laying them down in front of him. He got ready to snap, looked up and everything was clear and snapped the ball just as I was putting the ball down. It caught me right in the head. I got quite a shiner. The headline the next day was 'Young Mara first Giant Casualty.'"

Young Mara survived.

Years before that inadvertent knock on the head, an even younger Mara changed the way the Giants operated on game days.

"I was susceptible to colds," Mara said. "In 1925 the team bench was on the south side of the Polo Grounds, which was the shady side. I wanted to go sit down on the bench. The next day my mother told my father, 'Put the Giants on the sunny side so Well can sit on the bench.'"

No matter where they've called home ever since, the Giants bench has been positioned on the sunny side of the field.

Shape Up or Ship Out

Nowadays, players (if they know what's good for them) arrive at training camp in peak shape, as the byproduct of superior conditioning programs and huge salaries afford players time aplenty to sculpt their bodies.

This wasn't always the case. There was a time when players, under the hot sun of training camp, spent week after week shedding pounds and reawakening muscles, preparing for the grind of the season.

"That's where you had to get in shape," recalled Dick Lynch, a Giants cornerback from 1959-66. "In those days they'd give you a sheet of paper, do 10 of these, do this, run this, but we never used to. About a week before training camp, I put all that shit on me, the sweat clothes and started jogging. By the time I got up to training camp, I got on the scale, they'd say, 'Wow, you're in good shape.' I'd say, 'Yeah, I worked out.'"

Unlike Lynch, some of the linemen carried more than a few excess pounds and were forced to sweat off the extra tonnage. At times, it wasn't pretty.

"We were training up in Connecticut," Lynch said. "Rosey Grier, our defensive tackle, came into camp and he had this in his agreement with Wellington Mara, if he came in under 300 pounds he'd get $1,000 dollars a pound on his contract as a bonus. I think he ended the season somewhere around 275. He came into camp, they put him on the scale up in Fairfield, it went right to the top, and that was over 300. So they had to take him up to Bridgeport and put him on a truck scale. He weighed 350-something pounds, so they put him on a fruit diet.

"In 1960, the last game of the preseason we played in Los Angeles, and it was one of those hot days, like a steam bath. Rosey knew he was going to get a lot of work. As the game went on, the Rams recognized he was out of shape a little bit, every time they hit him the water came off him. It was a night game, and you could see the spray of the water. It looked like Niagara Falls. The guys were laughing and hollering at him, 'C'mon Rosey, hang in there.' They kept hitting him, they ran after him, he yelled to [defensive coordinator] Andy Robustelli, 'C'mon Andy, take a time-out.' And Andy says, 'We're with the defense, we don't take time-outs.'

"Rosey says, 'I got rights to call a time-out.' He said, 'Time-out, ref,' and just fell over on the ground. They took the water out there, we didn't get nothing, he poured it all on himself. And he's gasping for breath, he says, 'Ref, is there such a thing as two time-outs in a row?' "

Welcome Aboard

Y.A. Tittle, the Hall of Fame quarterback, spent two years in the All-American Conference, 11 with the 49ers in the NFL and had no reason to believe he wasn't headed toward a 12th year in

San Francisco. Tittle, 35 years old, did not anticipate anything special was about to happen when his 49ers on August 12, 1961, traveled to face the Giants in Portland, Oregon.

For the first half of the preseason game, Tittle knew he'd be on the bench, watching John Brodie start at quarterback. "He played the first half, and the Giants just killed him," Tittle said. "I mean, I think they were ahead 20-0 at halftime."

Brodie was crushed running the shotgun offense. Ah, Tittle figured, this is my chance to get the upper hand in the battle for the 49ers starting quarterback job. Tittle, operating out of the T-formation, got his chance in the second half, braced for the same ferocity from the Giants defense.

Tittle was not prepared for what he got.

"I came in the second half, and I thought I'd probably get the same treatment," Tittle said, "but no one touched me. I had perfect protection.

"I completed my first eight passes and we scored and then we got the ball back, Andy Robustelli hit me one time from the outside, and as I went down he grabbed me, picked me up, asked if I was OK. So I completed another pass. No pass rush. I had time to look here, look there, look everywhere.

"Sam Huff red-dogged through, he had a clean shot at me, somebody missed an assignment and he just veered off, didn't even make contact with me. I got to thinking, 'What are they doing? They're taking it easy on old quarterbacks, I guess.' We just ripped 'em apart, we won [21-20] and I scored the 21 points, so I figured I put Brodie on the bench and I'd have my job secured. I completed something like 19 of 23, and two of those were dropped. I'd just never had a day like that."

Feeling absolutely pleased with himself, a satisfied Tittle walked off the field.

Y.A. Tittle (Photo courtesy of the New York Giants)

"I go down into the tunnel in the stadium in Portland, Sam Huff ran up, shook my hand and congratulated me. He said right before the kickoff they finally finished the deal to trade me to New York and they didn't want any of their defensive players to lay a hand on me.

"Sam said, 'Allie [Sherman] told us we made a trade for you, don't rough him up. If you hurt him it's gonna cost you $1,000.'

So they didn't touch me and that was the best game of my entire life."

Two days later, 49ers coach Red Hickey officially informed Tittle he was headed to the Giants.

Looney, All Right

The Giants surely took a gamble in 1964 when they used their first-round draft pick to select Joe Don Looney, a highly talented but troubled running back out of Oklahoma. Ultimately, the gamble did not pay off, as Looney never played a game for the Giants. Despite his brief stay, anyone who ventured into Looneys orbit was not apt to forget him.

"He was 6-foot-2, 235, and we thought he was going to be the white Jimmy Brown," said Don Smith, the Giants public relations director at the time. "He was unbelievable as a football player. But he had beaten up an assistant coach at Oklahoma, punched out a professor in a class. He was a tremendously strong and mean guy, and nobody knew how to handle him, so I think a lot of the NFL clubs kind of figured this guy's trouble, but the Giants for some reason thought we could reform this guy. It took four guys to bring him down, but he had this history of emotional outbursts and attacks on people. He turned out to be an evil guy in camp."

His one and only training camp with the Giants was memorable and downright frightening.

"We had a policy after the lunch break," Smith said. "The press guys weren't allowed to go upstairs into the players' rooms because Allie Sherman didn't like the writers running around the halls, so the system was the writers would tell me who they wanted, I'd go up and get the guy and bring him down to the press room.

"One day somebody wanted Looney. I go up and knock on the door, I open the door, the room was completely dark, it's noontime, he's got all the shades down, he's sitting there and he's squeezing two rubber balls and he's watching these huge biceps pop up and down. He had his back to me. Before I could say anything he said, 'I don't know who is there, but you got five seconds to get out of here if you want to be alive much longer.' I got the hell out.

"I tell Sherman he won't come down. Sherman says, 'He won't, huh?' Up goes Allie. A minute later Allie comes down, a couple of shades paler, no Looney. Finally Wellington Mara went up, and Wellington didn't even get him out of there."

A few days later, the Giants unveiled a new piece of equipment, a tackling dummy and sled that had so much tension in its steel bands that often players would slam into it and get sent spiraling backward on the ricochet.

"It was always fun to watch guys hit it for the first time," Smith said.

The day came when it was time for the running backs to hit the sled. Everyone was anxious to see what would happen when Looney made contact.

"He came charging out there and hit this goddamn thing," Smith said. "Well, it flipped him back, one somersault back over his head, back in the dirt and everybody started to laugh. He got up and looked at every guy in the face, like, 'You laughing at me?' Everybody stopped laughing right away.

"Then he turned around and he ran full speed and he jumped on top of this sled and put his arms around this dummy that had knocked him down and he started kicking it and punching it and tried to rip it off the top of the sled. He was berserk. He was trying to kill the sled."

Everyone figured that was the end of Looney's attack on the tackling sled. But later that night, players inside their dorm rooms were awakened by an awful, eerie thudding sound from out on the practice field.

"There was Looney, in his jockey shorts, nothing else, and he had an ax handle and he was beating the dummy in the middle of the night out on the field. The guy was terrible."

Looney didn't last much longer. On August 25, 1966, the Giants traded him to the Colts.

Calling the Shots

The tradition under Alex Webster during training camp was for the coaching staff and writers to get together for some cocktails between the afternoon practice and dinner. It was called the 5:30 Club, and Webster was a willing and able host.

"We were down at Monmouth College [in 1972] and Alex liked to have a scotch or two," tight end Bob Tucker said. "Alex was always a little wobbly at dinner time. After dinner you had a meeting in one of the classrooms from 7 p.m. to 9 p.m. Like 7:15 the film would start. Alex comes barging in, it's about 20 after seven, he clicks the lights on and says, 'You guys still here? The problem with this team is nobody drinks enough beer. I want everybody out of here.' Closes down the meeting.

"With Alex, you had to read between the lines, you couldn't take literally what he said. You knew what he meant, that we needed a lot more camaraderie on the team, get the hell out of these meetings and go have some fun.

"One day he comes out at practice in the morning, the guys are dropping passes, missing blocks, jumping offside, blocking the wrong guys, it was just a disaster this particular morning. So halfway through he gets pissed off and he calls everybody up. 'Damn,' he says, he starts screaming at everybody, reading everybody the riot act. He says, 'Get off the field, and just for that, no practice this afternoon either!' So we had the afternoon off."

Enough Is Enough

No matter how grueling, players during training camp almost always fall in line and abide by the requirements put forth by the head coach. After all, he's the boss. Once, though, the rigors of camp became so unbearable that a revolt nearly took place on the practice fields of Pace University.

Ray Perkins arrived on the scene to coach the Giants in 1979, and immediately, players learned that life as they knew it was over. As a young veteran, defensive end George Martin thought he knew what an NFL training camp was all about, but as soon as Perkins took control, Martin and the other Giants received a punishing education.

Camp Perkins was no Club Med. Still, the Giants endured. But during the summer of 1980, Perkins decided to turn up the intensity.

"We had three-a-days under Ray Perkins," Martin said. "That was the training camp from hell. We had 16 knee surgeries that year in training camp. Three-a-days was unheard of, it was like the Bataan Death March, that's what we were calling it. These were full pads every day, hitting every day, full contact every day."

Martin considered himself to be in excellent shape but his body could not withstand the abuse.

"It was after our morning practice, I had gone into the cafeteria to get lunch," Martin said. "You lose ungodly sums of liquid, you'll lose eight to 10 pounds during a practice session. I came out of the lunchroom and I got a cramp in my right hand, and that cramp was like a river meandering through my body. It went up my right arm to my shoulder, to the other shoulder, down the left arm, back, just a total lock-up. Eventually I had to get some IV fluids in me."

Martin was not alone in his misery.

"I do not exaggerate, we would have at least three people leave in an ambulance every day, from every practice, morning and night, to up to six or seven," said quarterback Phil Simms, at the time entering his second season with the Giants. "In fact, some of the coaches, I've learned, would say, 'If we don't get six of 'em in this practice we haven't worked 'em hard enough.' I'd be on the practice field, that damn ambulance, I tell you, guys would be cramping up left and right. We'd have guys fall down in the lunch room and cramp and throw trays and just spasm out on the floor, it was incredible."

The grumbles grew louder and louder until the players had enough. "We finally had a mutiny," Martin said. "Jim Clack, our center, was the senior guy at that time, we all banded together and said, 'Hey, we're not gonna take this.'"

A confrontation ensued.

"Jim goes to meet with Ray Perkins, and I'm thinking this is great, we're gonna ease up a little," Simms said. "About five minutes later, Ray Perkins comes marching down the steps, kind of slams his little notebook on the podium, looks at all of us in the auditorium and says, 'Men, I don't give a fuck if every one of you leave, I'll go out and get 80 new guys right off the street and do better than you fucking guys are doing!' It was crushing. You know what, it got worse? He practiced us harder."

Eventually, with players dropping left and right, Perkins did relent . . . somewhat.

"Ray bowed to the pressure and rescinded the three-a-days," Martin said. "We stood in unison, because guys were getting hurt, careers were being lost, guys were being abused, it was just inhuman. I've never seen a group of guys band together so quickly against a tyrant, and that's exactly what he was at that time. Ray was there another year or two. We were not sorry to see him go."

Tough Sledding

With the second overall pick in the 1981 NFL Draft, the Giants selected Lawrence Taylor, making anything that happened in the next 11 rounds almost superfluous. Almost.

In the eighth round the Giants took a shot at a guard from Wake Forest named Billy Ard, who not only made the team but also earned a place in the starting lineup at left guard. He stayed there for seven consecutive years, making Ard one of the great investments in team history.

That same draft, the Giants in the second round took Dave Young, a bulky tight end from Purdue. Young was supposed to be a star, or at the very least a steady contributor. Unlike Ard, Young's stay was not long and he never came close to living up to, much less surpassing, his lofty draft status.

"We could have had Howie Long, we could have had a lot of guys, it was a great draft that year," Ard said. "Dave Young was like a slug. Big guy, talented, soft hands, nice guy.

"Our second year, Dave Young shows up at training camp, jumps on the scale, he's like eight pounds overweight. He had a really bad rookie year too, he broke his hand and he did nothing to distinguish himself as being anything but a bust. Then he comes in eight pounds overweight. Ray Perkins says, 'Son, you go home and get yourself in shape and I'll see you next week.'

"He comes back a week later, he's now 12 pounds overweight. We practice in the morning, it's a hot day, then we had a good, hard afternoon practice, and I remember I was going to lift weights, and there was Ray Perkins going over to Young. Perkins says, 'Dave Young, you stay afterwards.' Ray Perkins got on this two-man sled like he was Ben Hur and Dave Young had to take that sled, with Ray on it, and drive it up and down the football field. I mean, literally, drive it 100 yards up and 100 yards back.

"Then he just fell to the ground, passed out, basically. When Ray walked off the sled and Dave was down on the ground, I walked over and said, 'Young, you better suck it up son, because they're going to try to kill you.' Ray walked into the locker room and cut him that day. He had to torture him before he cut him. I'm saying to myself, 'That's the NFL, that's Ray Perkins.'"

Nice Place You've Got Here

At the time, he certainly did not know he was gaining valuable information and learning a worthwhile lesson. All Bill Parcells knew for certain was that the place was lousy.

Lousy is the mannerly description of the Giants' training camp setup from 1975-87 at Pace University in Pleasantville, New York, which sounds like an idyllic location but, in actuality, was anything but.

"The facilities, it's pretty hard to describe by today's standards how inferior they were," Parcells said. "We had one little building for offices, downstairs was a locker room, and in those days it had upwards of 100 guys down there in a locker room with 12 shower heads, six apiece on one shower. Only two six-headed showers, all the guys had to take showers there.

"There were three small tables that our training room could use. For practice we had a field and a half, but the big field was always soaked because it was below a rock embankment. Every time it would rain, the water would drain down off the rocks onto the field, and the field was usually 90 percent of the time unplayable. The other half field really wasn't half a field, it was like a downhill slope with a goalpost at the top next to that embankment, and the remaining 40 yards of the field went down toward that building we housed our offices in. But outside the building was a weight tent, so in reality the field was about 40 yards, but we had to be careful, because there were spikes holding the rope for the tent.

"We used to have a steamroller that would try to flatten the good field out so we could practice on it. Well, the steamroller got stuck in the middle of the field. It sunk. I mean it was about a foot down, so they couldn't get the steamroller out and they couldn't get a truck in there to tow it out because the truck would sink, so we had that half a field.

"The players would tell you about the goose shit. We used to go out to the field to stretch, and the Canadian geese used to fly over in the morning on that little half a field and they would crap all over the field, and by the time the players got out there, that's what they had to sit in. It was awful."

As bad as it was, Parcells learned something that he turned into one of his coaching axioms.

"What that taught me was that facilities meant nothing in football, because that was 1986, and that's when we won the Super Bowl. The players on the field, that's what counts."

Eye of the Storm

If you have to play in it, you might as well practice in it. That's the Bill Parcells mantra. If it's cold, big deal. Put on a sweatshirt and get going. A little rain never hurt anyone, either. But there was one particular weather condition that turned Parcells into a nervous wreck.

"One thing about training camps that always sticks out in my mind, Parcells was always deathly afraid of lightning," receiver Phil McConkey said. "We're at Pace University. If there was a lightning bolt reported in Morristown, New Jersey, we were going inside.

"One day it started to thunder and lightning, and Parcells was the first one off the field. We had this tent outside the practice fields and some guys are sitting inside this tent, it's a torrential downpour. Here comes LT [Lawrence Taylor] from the locker room. He's got a driver and a bunch of balls and some tees and he starts teeing the ball up. Parcells is cowering somewhere, in some bunker away from the lightning, and here's his star player out with a golf club in the middle of a lightning storm hitting drives."

Phone Home

The Giants in 1983 received an extra 12th-round draft pick from the Redskins, who won the Super Bowl the previous season. That meant the Giants owned the very last selection in the NFL Draft. They used it on a running back out of California named John Tuggle.

Tuggle earned a rare distinction: the label of Mr. Irrelevant, the tongue-in-cheek nickname foisted annually on the very last player taken. No previous Mr. Irrelevant had ever made the team that picked him in the draft.

As the 335th player chosen in the draft, Tuggle instantly became an enormous long shot to make the team. He arrived at training camp and immediately became the sort of player Bill Parcells, entering his first season as head coach, wanted on his roster. Tuggle was tough, hard-working, passionate, and what he lacked in ability and pure talent he made up for by doing anything and everything with an almost religious zeal.

"That preseason he was making his mark, and Parcells was looking for that kind of guy," said receiver Phil McConkey, that summer attending his first NFL training camp with the Giants.

Tuggle made it through the early rounds of cuts but remained no sure thing.

"It was the last preseason game and the guy was on the bubble, I'm standing on the sideline next to Parcells, the offense is on the field," McConkey said. "John Tuggle makes a devastating block on a running play, comes off the field towards the bench. Parcells takes his headset off, kind of greets him a couple of yards onto the field and he goes, 'Son, what a block! Here, call your wife.' He hands the kid the headset and says, 'Call your wife, tell her you made this team.'"

He made the team. Tuggle's career with the Giants came to a premature end when he died of cancer in 1986 at the age of 25.

He Ain't Heavy

If the truth hurts, it's probably better to lie. Or, at least fib a little. Especially dealing with Bill Parcells and his, well, shall we say, girth issue.

"We were up at training camp, and [Parcells] was getting bigger and bigger and bigger," said Ronnie Barnes, the Giants senior vice president of medical services and head trainer since 1980. "[Equipment manager] Eddie Wagner never gave him pants with the size in them. Parcells always thought he was a 36 or 38 because Eddie would fit him and snip all the sizes out. Parcells would say, 'Don't tell me the number.'

"One day we were at training camp at Pace and we're going from one practice field to the other, and in order to get there you had to go over a snow fence. Eddie and I are following Parcells up to that field and he, in a very unathletic way, jumps this snow fence. He turns around and says, 'What are you guys laughing about?'

"He always said, 'If I lost weight no one would know, it's like someone throwing a deck chair off the Queen Mary.' One day Eddie and I are talking to him, people think we're talking about equipment. Parcells sees a fan, he says, 'Be honest with me now, now don't look right now, but look over my right shoulder, you see that fat guy sitting there, he looks happy, he looks like he's enjoying practice?' He goes, 'I'm not that fat, am I?'

"Our answer was, 'Oh no, Coach.'"

Beating the Deadline

The last place Joe Morris figured he'd wind up was in New York as the 1982 NFL Draft unfolded and the Giants, in the first round, selected Butch Woolfolk, a running back from Michigan. But lo and behold, the Giants again opted for a running back in the second round, plucking Morris out of Syracuse.

"I asked [head coach] Ray Perkins, 'Why did you draft me?'" Morris said. "He said, 'Well, one of you guys is going to work out and one of you is not. It doesn't matter to me which one does.' I looked at him and thought, 'That's kind of nuts.'"

Sure enough, Perkins' words proved to be prophetic. Woolfolk never developed and was gone after three years. The short (5-foot-7) and stocky (195 pounds) Morris played his way into the starting lineup and in 1985 rushed for a team-high 1,336 yards and a franchise-record 21 touchdowns. Morris was better than the Giants anticipated and, as a reward, he wanted a new, more lucrative contract. The team was unwilling to meet Morris' price. And so, prior to the 1986 season, he showed up at training camp as a disgruntled worker.

"I talked to Bill Parcells and said, 'Look, I want my contract taken care of. I'll participate in all the no-contact drills until I get my contract signed,'" Morris said. "He agreed to that. He figured eventually I would just start practicing and not worry about it. It was fine the first couple of weeks. Then Bill called me into his office and said, 'We got a preseason game, plus we're gonna practice against the Falcons for a week.' He said to me, 'If you're coming to Atlanta it's going to have to be full-go.' I said, 'No, you know what you told me.' He said, 'I'm sending you home then.' I said, 'OK, fine.'

"The Giants sent me a letter saying I left camp. I said, 'No, the coach sent me out.' When the team was in Atlanta I got a call from all my teammates asking what the hell I was doing. I said, 'Look, guys, I'm trying.' I go back to camp with the understanding that my contract is going to be done before the season. I say if it's not done before the season I might miss the first game.

Phil McConkey (AP Images)

"We fly down to Dallas for the season opener. Phil Simms drives by my house to make sure I left to come to the game because he wasn't sure I'd get on the plane. Before the game Parcells said, 'Is your contract done?' I told him no. He said, 'Are you playing?' I said, 'If my contract's not done, no, I'm not gonna play.' He said, 'I'm pissed off at you.' I said, 'Bill, you didn't need to be involved in this. You should have just let it go.'

"I called my agent from a payphone. He said, 'The deal is done, it's set, you get taped and have the best game of your life.' I said, 'All I want to know is if it's a fair deal.' He said, 'It's the best deal we're gonna get, Joe, unless you want to miss a game.' I said, 'I don't want to miss a game.'

"Bill said, 'You're gonna play like shit because your mind's not focused.' I told him, 'I guarantee you this: I don't give a damn if they have Tony Dorsett and Herschel Walker, check our stats at the end of the game. See who has the better game.' Sure enough, I had 87 yards and a touchdown and I think they had like 88 [actually 89] rushing yards but they did win the game. I played my heart out.

"I think there were some hurt feelings, some people who were mad about it, some people who held grudges."

One-Eyed Wonder

Players must play in pain. That's the rule in the NFL, but rarely does that rule apply on the second day of training camp.

Unless Bill Parcells is roaming the sideline.

The Giants in the summer of 1987 were coming off their first Super Bowl triumph, and one day into training camp at Pace University, Phil McConkey got poked in the eye during practice. An errant fingernail scratched McConkey's cornea and his eye swelled shut, making him, in effect, a one-eyed punt returner and receiver.

"I got my sweaty T-shirt on and still have my pants on with the pads," McConkey said. "Our trainer, Ronnie Barnes, took me in his car to see some local eye doctor. They figure out what it was, put some ointment in my eye and put a patch over my right eye. By the time all this is said and done the afternoon practice was about to start, the team was out stretching as we pulled up in the car."

McConkey figured he'd at the very least get the afternoon off, especially with the scent of a Super Bowl victory still sweetening the air.

"I had never taken my pads off, I had never taken a shower, I had grabbed a sandwich at 7-11 on the way back," McConkey said. "Anywhere else, any other team, any other coach in that situation, you'd at least sit out the afternoon practice and maybe the next day or two until you get your vision back. Well, that's not happening with Bill Parcells. You got to practice. He didn't say to me, 'You better go out and practice.' I just knew better, me being on the fringe my whole career."

Taking the field as a one-eyed wonder was no fun.

"My whole career Parcells stood next to me, every punt," McConkey said. "Every catch was never good enough. I used to be able to throw two balls in the air, catch the ball that was punted, catch the two balls I threw up, stuff the balls in my pants, catch 'em behind my back, it was never good enough for him. He criticized me every single catch, which pissed me off to no end, but forced me to focus like nobody's business.

"I'm catching all these punts seeing out of one eye and I drop one and he's just jumping all over me, 'Catch the damn ball!' There's no excuses accepted with this guy. I knew it before, but I knew it even more then. That's how he got the most out of me or anybody else."

Might Parcells not have known that McConkey, even though his eye was covered with a patch, was debilitated?

"Not have known?" McConkey wondered. "I looked like a freaking pirate!"

The Prankster

They were coming. He knew they were coming. And, no matter how fiercely he resisted, quarterback Kent Graham knew there was no way he could avoid receiving his inevitable punishment.

Graham learned soon enough from the likes of Phil Simms and Jeff Hostetler that as a rookie, there was an initiation he had to endure in order to be accepted by his peers. Pleasant? No. Necessary? Yes.

On the last night of training camp, 1992, Graham sensed something was about to go down. "I was thinking, 'They're all going to come get me,' and I was right. I barricaded myself in my room and Hostetler came into my room from the second floor window. He got caught up in the metal blinds. You could hear them clank. Somehow Jeff got up on the second floor with a ladder, and I woke up out of a deep sleep, it was like two in the morning and I'm thinking, 'They're coming in!'

"Jeff was caught in the window, so I started to push him out. Then I'm thinking, 'Wait a minute, I can't do that, this guy's worth a lot of money, he's my teammate.' He was our starting quarterback at the time. We wrestled, he got in the window, un-barricaded my room, and then all of the guys who were waiting outside my room, they tied me up, poured orange juice and shaving cream on all my clothes, duct-taped me up in my underwear outside with [fellow rookie quarterback] Dave Brown. Both of us knew we were going to get pounded. It was things like that where you took your beating and then you were part of the group. It made the team special. That was part of the tradition. I learned from some of the best ones, Phil and Hoss and Bart Oates were always some of the best practical jokers. I kind of carried on that tradition."

Oates, the team's devilish starting center, was a master prankster. Once, Graham flipped on the air conditioner in his Honda Accord and a terrible stench blew out of the vents. "Somebody put some kind of skunk in my motor," Graham said. "I think it was Bart who did it to me."

Another time, Oates messed with strength and conditioning coach Johnny Parker. "He got him with this DMSO stuff," Graham said. "It's a chemical agent you put on your skin, it will take whatever's on your skin and take it immediately into the bloodstream. A lot of guys in the old days used to take the DMSO, put it on their joints, you put some anti-inflammatory on your skin and then rub the DMSO on it. They used to use it for horses. It would give you really bad breath, kind of a garlicky taste in your mouth.

"Bart put some DMSO in Johnny Parker's cologne. He split it half and half. So Johnny would slap it on his face in the morning and he'd have DMSO breath. I remember telling Johnny, 'Your breath smells terrible, man.' He'd say, 'You know Kent, my wife has been saying my breath has been kicking a bit.' Johnny kept slapping it on every morning. Bart was one of the best ones ever."

Graham learned at the feet of the master, inhaled the knowledge, and turned it loose on others. Graham became one of the most feared Giants when it came to conjuring up ways to harass the rookies. His favorite mode of abuse: Secret powder.

Graham was turned onto the stuff by George Sefcik, the running backs coach. "It's an FBI powder they put on counterfeit money," Graham explained. "You put any speck of it in somebody's sock, you get any water, any perspiration on it whatsoever it will explode purple on you."

Kent Graham (AP Images)

When he craved some variation, Graham would take a heat-inducing balm and spread it inside the underwear of younger teammates. "You had to be real selective with who you messed with, guys who would take it in good stride," he said.

One of Graham's proudest moments? Torturing Phil Simms.

"At training camp at Fairleigh Dickinson, they'd always give us parking tickets," Graham said. "I remember Phil one time got a ticket. I kept on taking that same ticket and kept putting it on his car, and he kept thinking he was getting like four, five parking tickets. He kept getting mad and ticked off, he's like, 'I can't believe they got me again.' I just kept on replacing the same ticket."

Chapter  2

THE SEASON

Clash of Titans

Jim Brown lived to run with the ball. Sam Huff lived to stop the run. When these two Hall of Fame dynamos collided, Lord help anyone unfortunate enough to venture into the path of destruction.

"One time in New York he ran through everybody, I mean he went like about 75 yards, and it was unreal," Huff said. "He was known throughout the league as 'The Big Man' and brother, he could run over you."

The rivalry was born in college when Huff at West Virginia went against Brown's Syracuse team. In one encounter, Huff attempted to tackle Brown and came away with four broken teeth and a nasty scar on his nose.

Huff came to relish these challenges.

"He's the greatest," Huff said. "I like to play angry, I was an angry player, at linebacker you have to be. He would psyche you, he would get up and pat you on the back and say, 'That was a nice tackle, Big Sam.' I would say, 'Leave me alone, don't talk to me.'

"We had a defense that could take a ballplayer and shut him down, I don't care who he was. We shut Jim Brown down. No other defense has ever done that against Jim Brown."

It happened. You can look it up. In the Eastern Conference playoff game on December 21, 1958, the Giants swarmed all over Brown and the Cleveland Browns, winning in a shutout, 10-0. Brown had a career-low eight yards and ran the ball only seven times as eventually it made no sense to keep sending him into the line against the ravenous Giants defense.

"I knocked him out, right at the pitcher's mound at Yankee Stadium," Huff said. "Dick Modzelewski hit him low, and Jim Brown was trying to shake him off and I came in and drilled him and hit him and dinged him. He said he wasn't knocked out, I said, 'You might as well have been.' I tell everybody he was knocked out. I tell you what, he was a great sportsman on the field. He really was. He was a pleasure to play against, but he was also scary to play against."

The Young Man and the Author

The last place Frank Gifford, born in Santa Monica, raised in Bakersfield, and a star at the University of Southern California, figured he'd wind up was New York.

"I came just for a year to see what it was like," he said, "and stuck around forever."

Gifford was the Giants' first-round draft pick in 1952, and soon enough, he was introduced to the glitz and glamour of New York City.

"The first thing I did was get one suit and one tie," Gifford said. "[Head coach] Steve Owen, whom I was never terribly fond of, invited me to have dinner with him one night at Toots Shor's. So I took my wife, and he and his wife and Toots came up and it was like I'd known him all my life. It's the only place I went for the first couple of years. I never had to pay the check. I'd always pretend to try hard to pay it, but he wouldn't let me. He probably knew we didn't have any money."

Often on Monday afternoons, Gifford would head over to Toots Shor's for a quiet (and, hopefully, inexpensive) lunch.

"I came in one day," Gifford said, "and he said, 'You by yourself?' I said, 'Yeah.' He said, 'Why don't you sit with a friend of mine?' And I had lunch with Ernest Hemingway.

"He was in town to watch a fight, he was doing an article on Ingemar Johansson, who was fighting at the Polo Grounds. He was curious about football, he was making all kinds of analogies between that and bullfighting and boxing. We talked about the difference between a team sport and an individual sport. He loved physicality, that's what he always wrote about.

"It was just like talking to a guy from Bakersfield. It was hard to imagine that was happening to me."

Gifford passed away on August 9, 2015, at age 84.

Worth 1,000 Words

At the time, all Y.A. Tittle could do was hope to keep breathing as jolts of pain filled his chest muscles. Little did the tough Giants quarterback know that such a difficult moment would be frozen in time by the flash of a camera.

The famous black and white photo of Tittle, sunk to his knees, bald and bleeding from his head, looking dazed and confused, hangs in the Pro Football Hall of Fame in Canton, Ohio. It is one of the great symbols of hard-hitting football, a picture that encapsulates the rugged nature of the sport in the mid-'60s.

"It retired me," Tittle said of the physical damage he suffered that day.

Y.A. Tittle (AP/Images)

On September 20, 1964, one week before his 38th birthday, Tittle, against the Steelers at Pitt Stadium, threw a screen pass to the left side intended for Frank Gifford. Tittle was pummeled by John Baker, the Steelers' 270-pound defensive end.

"He hit me just as I was releasing the ball, I didn't see him, he caught me under the armpits and sort of picked me up, his helmet was in my chest," Tittle said. "I was sort of gored like a bull, the picture looked so bad, it looks like my face is all cut up. Well, that was just where my facemask cut me."

The ball floated into the air and was intercepted by defensive tackle Chuck Hinton, who returned it eight yards for a touchdown. Pittsburgh won the game 27-24.

The impact of Baker's hit caused Tittle's helmet to fly off as he dropped to his knees. The blood streaming down his face was gruesome but not dangerous. Far more serious was the concussion, the badly bruised ribs, and the damage to his chest muscles.

Morris Berman, a photographer from the *Pittsburgh Post Gazette*, took the historic picture. Tittle was able to play again, but not effectively, and called it quits following that season.

And what of John Baker, the man who inflicted all the pain and suffering?

"He ran for sheriff in North Carolina, he was the first black sheriff to get elected in his county," Tittle said. "He took that picture of me and put it up on about 1,500 telephone poles and under the picture was the saying, 'If you don't obey the law this is what Big John's gonna do to you.' I went back to North Carolina and helped him kick off his campaign."

Bednarik's Blast

When Frank Gifford began going out with Kathy Lee, he warned her of a certain incident in his past that he knew would resurface.

"I remember telling her, 'One thing you're going to hear almost every day of your life, especially when we get around football people, is [Chuck] Bednarik,'" Gifford said. "She said, 'What's that, a pasta?' She had no clue who he was."

She learned soon enough. Pictures don't lie.

Or do they?

There's a famous black-and-white shot of a prone Gifford laid out on the Yankee Stadium grass, flat on his back, his right leg bent slightly at the knee, looking as if he might be dead. Standing over him, ala a young Muhammad Ali glowering over the defeated Sonny Liston, is Bednarik, wearing his familiar No. 60 Eagles jersey, thrusting a fist into the air in celebration.

Legend has it that Bednarik punctuated the devastating hit on Gifford on November 20, 1960, by shouting, "This fucking game is over!" That's how Bednarik actually signed copies of the picture.

Legend also has it that Gifford, as a result of the vicious collision in a 17-10 loss, did not play again for two years.

"Oh, that's kind of all silly," Gifford said. "He knows better than that, too. He actually perpetuates it himself, and it's kind of sad. He was so much better than just a guy who knocked me out of a game."

True, Gifford did miss the final four games that year and sat out the 1961 season, but not because of Bednarik's blast.

"It's ridiculous, it's one of the comedies of that end of the game, the spectacular as opposed to the reality," Gifford said. "A lot of people think that he knocked me out of the game and I never played again. I came back and played three more years and went to the Pro Bowl at a third position, at receiver. I ended my football career for a year myself because I had two kids, I was working in television every night.

"After I took that year off, not because of the injury, my kids were all in school at that time, I was working for CBS, I had a terrific job, and I realized midway through that next season, hell, I can still play this game."

For the record, Bednarik's punishing hit did leave Gifford with a concussion.

"I was unconscious for a little bit, not too long," Gifford said. "There was such drama involved in it. I remember being in the locker room, there was a cop who died, I guess, the cop had died at the game, they brought him in and laid him right next to me. He was on one table, I was on the other, and I hear these people mumbling, 'He's gone,' and I'm listening to this, and I know they're not talking about me. I remember waking up in the hospital, thinking, 'This is a nice place to be,' so I stayed about a week."

The Trading Game

He never wanted to leave. Not ever. Sam Huff was drafted by the Giants in 1956 and by the time he left following the 1963 sea-

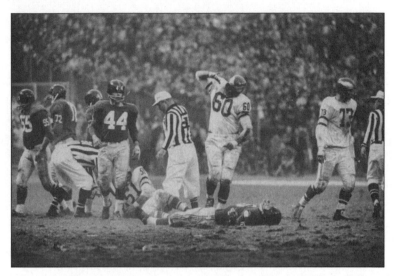

*Chuck Bednarik (60) looms over a motionless Frank Gifford. (John
G. Zimmerman/Time Life Pictures/Getty Images)*

son, he compiled enough credentials at middle linebacker to earn a
place in the Hall of Fame. Huff remains bitter that he didn't retire
as a Giant.

"Getting traded by the Giants was the most ridiculous thing
that ever happened, it never made any sense," Huff said. "They
traded away Dick Modzelewski, Erich Barnes, Rosey Grier, one
of the great defenses ever put together. Why? Because of head
coach Allie Sherman. He was no good to do that. He destroyed the
Giants, he destroyed all of us."

Privately, some believed that near the end of his Giants' run,
Huff was losing a step and growing into too much of a celebrity.
The company line at the time was that the Giants' defense was get-
ting old and worn.

"I took on an older club," Sherman explained. "That club had
been together four, five years. I had to make moves when I became
the head coach that were based on what reach I thought each man

still had. I examined the inventory. It was a good team, but even my owners acknowledged that maybe it was time for rebuilding."

That reasoning never sat well with Huff.

"That's bullshit," he exclaimed. "We could play. We shut down the Chicago Bears in the 1964 Championship Game when [Sherman's] offense that he coached turned the ball over seven times. He dismantles us. Why? We were not his defensive unit. Tom Landry designed us and put us together, and he was jealous of that. In my opinion, Allie Sherman wanted all the credit for the Giants being as good as we were."

Huff was sent to Washington in exchange for defensive tackle Andy Stynchula, running back Dick James, and a fifth-round draft pick. Huff spent the last five years of his career in Washington, but in his heart he remained a Giant.

"I've never gotten over it," Huff said. "Never. They didn't trade Frank Gifford. They didn't trade Charlie Conerly. They didn't trade Roosevelt Brown. They didn't trade anybody off the offense. Just all the defense."

Two years after he was traded away, Huff exacted his revenge when his Redskins whipped the Giants 72-41 in Washington on November 27, 1966. The Giants that season allowed a league-record 501 points.

"We scored 72 in Washington . . . I made sure of that," Huff said. "[Sherman] had it coming, I mean, he had it coming. We put that ball right where the sun doesn't shine."

In that game, the Redskins, leading 69-41, kicked a field goal with seven seconds remaining, as coach Otto Graham actually called a time-out before sending Charlie Gogolak onto the field.

"Allie Sherman went out of his mind and Graham's excuse was, 'Well, I thought he needed a little more work on his kicking,'" said Ed Croke, at the time a Giants public relations assistant. "The guy just kicked 11 extra points!"

Sam Huff (Francis Miller/Time Life Pictures/Getty Images)

Huff had the last laugh. It was Huff who called for the kicking unit to take the field and he could be heard shouting, "Field goal . . . field goal!" in the closing minute.

Hurts So Good

Great games have a way of sneaking up on players. Y.A. Tittle's most prolific game almost never happened.

Early in the 1962 season Tittle suffered a painful injury during a 17-14 victory over the Lions, a contusion on the right side of his body, affecting his right shoulder and right arm. There was every reason to believe Tittle would not be able to start at quarterback the following week against the Redskins.

"I didn't throw all week," Tittle said. "I practiced, but I didn't throw the ball. I was scared as hell."

As game time arrived on October 28, Tittle doubted he could go. "Allie Sherman said take it easy, go out and warm up, see what you think," Tittle said. "Well, I learned a long time ago that when a coach says, 'Can you play?' you'd better play. You CAN play. I mean, otherwise other guys would get in and do better than you and you're gonna create a problem."

He played, although he started slowly, carefully, not wanting to clue the Washington defense in that he was hurting. "I didn't throw downfield hardly at all until my arm really got to feeling good and I got confident," Tittle said.

After misfiring on his first seven passes, Tittle completed 12 straight. He threw for 505 yards, which at the time set a Giants record. The points came fast and furious. He finished with seven touchdown passes, a franchise record that still stands. The Giants routed the Redskins 49-34.

"I got on a hot streak," Tittle said modestly. "Everything I threw went for a touchdown. And I wasn't supposed to play."

"My Last Hit"

No one had to inform cornerback Dick Lynch that football was a brutal and at times dangerous business. He was paralyzed for about two minutes in 1957 while playing for Notre Dame in a historic game against Oklahoma. Lynch actually returned to score the lone touchdown in a 7-0 Irish victory that ended the Sooners' record 47-game winning streak.

That chilling memory served him well during the 1966 opener as the Giants embarked on the worst season in their history, a 1-12-1 disaster. Playing in Pittsburgh, the Giants and Steelers battled to a rare 34-34 tie as Lynch unexpectedly confronted the possible end of his career.

"I hit some receiver, instead of going out of bounds he decided to get another yard on me," Lynch said. "You just didn't think about whacking guys back then, I just wanted to hit him out, so I let up. Pinched my nerve back there."

Lynch couldn't move any part of his body below the waist. He also couldn't move his arms.

"Doc Sweeney came out and I said, 'Doc it happened once before, it will come back,'" Lynch said. "He kept asking me, 'Do you feel this? Do you feel this?' He keeps asking me. I keep answering, 'No, no, no.' They just slid me over and kept the game going."

For 10 minutes, Lynch was laid out, paralyzed. Instantly, he feared the worst. "Right on the sidelines I was thinking about Roy Campanella," he said. "I loved Roy, I was a Dodgers fan. I said 'Please God, don't let happen to me what happened to Roy.'"

Gradually, the feeling started to return to Lynch's extremities. The hit put Lynch out of action for a month. He returned to the field, briefly, to play some at safety, but was never the same. He retired following the season. The paralysis never completely faded away, as Lynch suffered a permanent deficiency of about 20 percent on the left side of his body. It forced him to switch his golf swing from right-handed to left-handed.

"It was time to quit after that, no doubt about it," he said. "I'm glad I made the decision not to go back, or else I'd be sitting in a wheelchair. It was my last hit, basically."

To the Moon, Y.A.

There's no place like New York, especially when you're winning.

"I played 14 years and at the end of my road went to New York during the '60s. The Yankees were winning, *The Sound of Music* and *My Fair Lady* were going on, and we were winning too," quarterback Y.A. Tittle said. "What a dream. The whole town was just electrified with sports and entertainment."

After spending the bulk of his career with the 49ers in San Francisco, Tittle was traded in 1961 to the Giants and fell in love with the bright lights of the big city.

"P.J. Clarke's, the 21 Club, you couldn't help but feel like a celebrity," Tittle said. "New Yorkers really did honor their sports stars. It was just so great. To be big somewhere else is nothing. To be big in New York is big."

One night, Tittle learned just how big.

"I'm sitting at Toots Shor's, Toots was going around meeting everybody, he asked me if I wanted to go visit Jackie Gleason,"

Dick Lynch (Photo courtesy of the New York Giants)

Tittle said. "I said yes. I went over, Jackie Gleason asked me to sit down. I had a beer with him, a couple of kids came over to the table and one said, 'Hey Mr. Tittle, can I get your autograph?' I said, 'Sure, son,' and I signed it. The kid turned to Jackie Gleason and said, 'Do you play tackle?' Jackie Gleason said, 'Get out of here you punk kids.' That says a lot about sports in New York."

One and Only Homer

An opposing defensive back once complained that it was unfair to expect him to cover Homer Jones, considering Jones himself did not know where he was going. Fran Tarkenton would call for a 12-yard square-out, Jones would run an 80-yard fly pattern. Jones was the quintessential home run receiver, capable of bringing a defense to its knees with a spectacular touchdown and equally as capable of bringing his teammates to tears with an unbelievable drop.

Jones holds the franchise record for the longest pass play in team history, and had a then-team record 98-yard reception from Earl Morrall against the Steelers in 1966. Jones owns the Giants' record with a career average gain of 22.6 yards per catch. He led the entire NFL with 14 touchdowns in 1967.

And Jones probably was among the league leaders in anecdotes told about him.

"He was one of the great characters of all time," said Don Smith, the Giants public relations director from 1960-73. "Homer was a nice little southern guy, nothing bothered Homer, World War III could be going on, and he wouldn't even know it. He was just in a state of perpetual bliss and the outside world had no effect on him."

Once, the threat of a transit strike in New York presented potential commuter problems for the Giants. "A lot of our players lived around town and came to Yankee Stadium for practice by subway," Smith said. "Allie Sherman said to me one day, 'I want you to go around and check with every player, make sure they have an alternate means of getting here.' He didn't want some guy to use the excuse of a subway strike to not be at practice at nine o'clock.

"I go down, Homer is sitting at his locker and I go, 'Homer, there's gonna be a transit strike tomorrow, and the coach is worried you might not be able to get here.' He says, 'That's all right, I take the subway.'"

The Race That Never Was

At 6-foot-3 and 240 pounds, Homer Jones was a physical specimen who played receiver for the Giants with varying degrees of effectiveness. No one, though, could ever question his blazing speed. He anchored the Texas Southern 400-meter relay team, helping to set a world record. Jones couldn't always hold on to the ball, but he could fly.

"I once had an idea of putting together a match race between Homer and Bob Hayes of the Cowboys at the Cotton Bowl," said Don Smith, the Giants public relations director during Jones' career (1964-69) in New York. "Hayes was the world's fastest human, and I figured in full football gear, in pads and a helmet, and carrying the ball, Homer's gonna beat this guy, because he's so much bigger and stronger.

"I had gotten some support for this, I had this moving toward a conclusion when Tom Landry stepped in."

Landry, the former Giants defensive coordinator, was the head coach of the Cowboys. He was not a man interested in frivolities.

"Landry was a good friend of mine, and he pulled me aside and said, 'Don, I'm not gonna let this happen,'" Smith said. "He said, 'We got Bob Hayes and he's advertised as the world's fastest man, I ain't gonna have him lose to Homer Jones in the Cotton Bowl, for you or anybody else.' So the great match race of the century never came off."

Traveling Men

During a relatively narrow (1970-77) slice of time, tight end Bob Tucker was involved in an uncommonly transient period in Giants history.

Tucker started out playing home games at Yankee Stadium, spent two years (1973-74) at the Yale Bowl in New Haven, Connecticut, one year (1975) at Shea Stadium—the home of the Mets and Jets in Flushing, New York—before finally landing at brand-new Giants Stadium in East Rutherford, New Jersey.

Understandably, Tucker adored playing in Yankee Stadium, with its rich history. He does not have the same fond memories of life at the Yale Bowl.

"It was a college field, and there was no barrier between the fans and the field," Tucker said. "That was OK for college, but for professional, it was not."

It got so bad that often, uninvited guests would find their way onto the field.

"Here it is the second quarter, and I'm standing on the sideline," Tucker said. "The defense is out on the field and there was no security, minimal, maybe one guy on the sideline saying, 'You can't come down on the field,' and I'd have some teenager standing right next to me, and he wants my chinstrap. I said, 'You got to wait until after the game here, I'm gonna need this for another hour or so.' Looking for souvenirs during the game. Amazing."

These were lean years for the Giants, who went 2-11-1 in 1973 to signal the end of Alex Webster's time as head coach. The next year, they were 2-12 in Bill Arnsparger's first season. The Giants were 1-11 playing at the Yale Bowl during those two seasons.

"We were an inept team offensively, defensively, and every-thing else, and it was sad," Tucker said. "You'd come out after the game, players would get on the bus and the fans used to push the bus sideways, the bus would rock, I mean, I'm telling you, I figured the bus was going over a couple of times. The fans, it was near riot-ous. These fans were pissed off. We didn't even put an entertaining product on the field. It was a shit show."

Baiting a Trade

There was nothing Bob Tucker had against John McVay, the man. Nothing at all.

"A great guy, a gentleman," Tucker said. "I couldn't say any-thing derogatory about him, but again, as a head coach, what did he know about football?"

As a talented pass-catching tight end, Tucker endured plenty of hardships during his stay with the Giants. There wasn't enough winning, but he adored playing for Alex Webster. He struggled deal-ing with the losing under Bill Arnsparger and realized soon enough that the failure was not going to cease with McVay calling the shots.

McVay came to the Giants from the Memphis Southmen of the World Football League and took over for Arnsparger midway through the 1976 season. The Giants won three of their last five games, and just like that, McVay became the full-time head coach.

Bob Tucker (Photo courtesy of the New York Giants)

"There were a lot of high spirits going on," Tucker said. "The Giants recognized this guy McVay must be a helluva coach. In reality it wasn't because McVay was the head coach, it was because Arnsparger wasn't."

Tucker couldn't take seeing a slew of former Memphis personnel infiltrating the Giants' locker room, posing as NFL players and coaches. Suddenly, the tight end was no longer a target in the passing game, and Tucker was relegated to working with the offensive line during practice, banished from the seven-on-seven passing drills.

"I remember the line coach, Jay Fry, he had this five-man sled he must have gone to sleep with every night, he brought it from Memphis, and what you did in practice for almost the entire time was either walk on your hands and do these calisthenics or go over and push the sled. I wish they paid me by the mile on that sled.

"One day I had it up to here, I told him to stick his sled and I went over to the seven-on-seven. I'm a real renegade now. They're surprised to see a tight end show up. I say, 'Let's go run some pass plays.' They didn't know what to do, John McVay's standing there, he said something and I guess I kind of rebuked him. He called me in at the end of the day and told me I was being disruptive. Disruptive? I want to win. I'm here to make money, you're costing me money. I want to get to the playoffs. I want to be on TV in the postseason, not sitting home watching it. It was just crazy."

It was part of a plan devised by Tucker to force a trade, as he couldn't stomach playing for the Giants any longer. He made the request to the general manager, Andy Robustelli, who did not react kindly.

"I said to Andy, 'I only have a short career, we're going nowhere, can you trade me?'" Tucker said. "He took a step backward and said, 'We're not trading you, who do you think you are?' So I figured the only way for me to get traded was to become a nuisance, a malcontent."

Finally, on October 24, 1977, on the eve of the trading deadline, Tucker was sent to the Vikings.

"I didn't enjoy being the malcontent, the renegade," Tucker said. "I felt bad for Wellington Mara. That's a cloud that hangs over me, I didn't want to be that way. But there was no other way for me to get out of there. I went out to Minnesota with Bud Grant for four years and made the playoffs every year, and I was back in the football business, just like I was with Alex Webster. It was like dying and going to heaven."

School's Out

Anyone who made an emotional investment in the Giants knows where they were on November 19, 1978. There were many, many dark days in the history of the franchise, but all pale in comparison to the day and the play simply and infamously known in Giants circles as "The Fumble." For the Philadelphia Eagles, it's forever dubbed "The Miracle at the Meadowlands."

The play is high on the list of all-time sports gaffes. The Giants held a 17-12 lead on the Eagles and, after intercepting a Ron Jaworski pass, had the game in hand. With 31 seconds left, all quarterback Joe Pisarcik had to do was kneel down twice and the clock would expire.

Pisarcik, though, carried out the running play sent in, never cleanly got the handoff into the hands of fullback Larry Csonka. The ball deflected off Csonka's hip, dropped to the turf, and was scooped up on one bounce by cornerback Herman Edwards, who ran untouched 26 yards for the touchdown that gave the Eagles an incredible 19-17 victory.

"At that time I was in law school at Fordham, and on game days I used to work in the TV booth as a spotter," said John Mara, son of owner Wellington Mara. "The broadcasters for that game were Don Criqui and Sonny Jurgensen. I can remember watching that play unfold and watching Herman Edwards run with the ball, and I slammed my fist down on the table, which some people have said I am prone to do.

"The electronic equipment, the microphones fell off the table, all the wires fell off the table. It was probably as upset as I've ever been in my life, and I think that was the last time they ever asked me to spot one of those games."

That wasn't the worst of it.

"I was sitting in the law library, the next day," Mara said, "and this one professor I had, who was kind of a wiseass, he was somebody that would tease me from time to time about the performance of the Giants, he kind of pointed at me, laughed at me and were it not for a friend of mine sitting next to me, restraining me, I think I would have killed him. Thank God I didn't. I never would have gotten my degree, much less been admitted to the bar."

Two weeks later, angry fans burned their season tickets outside Giants Stadium. The next week, fans hired a small plane to fly over the stadium, carrying a banner that read "15 Years of Lousy Football . . . We've Had Enough." Head coach John McVay was fired at season's end. As a franchise, the Giants were close to mortally wounded.

A Rookie's Fear

Running back Billy Taylor was a product of a high-scoring Texas Tech program, meaning when he arrived as a rookie in 1978, he was wholly unprepared for the prehistoric offensive setup he encountered with the Giants.

What he saw confounded him.

"The guy who was offensive coordinator when I got there was Bob Gibson, he was the worst offensive coordinator I've ever seen, and I was only a rookie," Taylor said. "I was thinking 'This can't be right,' because he was like pulling plays out of a hat, there was no rhyme or reason to what he did."

Knowledge of Gibson's incompetence was rampant inside the Giants' locker room.

"Joe Pisarcik decided he was going to call his own plays, so to speak, change the plays whenever he wanted to," Taylor said. "Then he got admonished by Gibson, who just totally dissed him in a meeting. Then it culminated in Joe not calling his own play when that fumble came off."

"That fumble" became "The Fumble," one of the darkest plays in Giants history, when Gibson, with the Giants leading 17-12, called for a handoff in the final 31 seconds against the Eagles. Pisarcik never got the ball to fullback Larry Csonka and Philadelphia cornerback Herman Edwards returned the fumble for the game-winning touchdown. Gibson was fired the following day.

"Joe didn't change the play like he should have, when the coach tells you to hand off with seconds left in the game, you really should just take it and fall on it," Taylor said. "Everyone was telling him that, but Joe didn't do it."

Years later, Pisarcik said, "The play never should have been called. [Gibson] should have just shut his mouth."

Standing on the sideline at the 35-yard line during that fateful play, Taylor said he was "in shock," but what followed in the manic locker room was even more troubling.

"It was total chaos," Taylor said. "I had never been that scared in a football game. I put my helmet on when I got into the locker room, because Harry Carson was throwing his stuff, John Mendenhall was too. I remember Jack Gregory was throwing stuff. It was just scary. I know I almost got hit by at least two helmets. If I got hit it really would have messed me up. There was so much stuff throwing around, it wasn't like a locker room, it was like you were in a war zone or something. I had never been in a situation like that, I didn't know what to do. It just culminated to me what had gone on all season."

A Punt to Remember

For 11 consecutive seasons, Dave Jennings was the be-all and end-all when it came to punting and the Giants. Jennings punted 931 times for the Giants, a team record, for 38,792 yards, also a team record.

No one could recall every one of those punts. One of them, though, stands out above all others.

The Giants were 8-7 back on December 19, 1981, seeking to end a horrendous stretch for the franchise: No playoff appearances since 1963. To finally end that dreary 17-year drought, the Giants needed to win their Saturday afternoon game against the Cowboys at Giants Stadium and hope the Packers lost to the Jets the next day.

It was one of those windy, brutal days in New Jersey, with the Giants and Cowboys tied at 10 heading into overtime. Leon Bright, the Giants' kick returner, took the kickoff out of his own end zone and got no farther than the five-yard line. Three offensive plays gained only five yards. It was fourth-and-five from the Giants' 10-yard line as Jennings trotted out onto the field, with a 35-mile-an-hour wind blowing back into his face.

"I was running down towards the tunnel end of the stadium where we came out," Jennings said, "and I said to myself, 'If this doesn't go well, I can just turn around and run through the tunnel and nobody will see me.' I hit a very good punt."

He sure did. The punt traveled 47 yards, somehow cutting through the wind, a credit to Jennings' attention to detail as he plied his craft. The punt pinned the Cowboys deep in their territory, the Giants took advantage of the ensuing field position, and won 13-10. The Jets beat the Packers the next day. The Giants were in the playoffs.

"I'm very proud of that punt," he said. "I've still got it on tape. I'm going to transfer it to DVD as soon as I can."

Some Friend

Of all the defensive linemen he knocked heads with, Giants guard Billy Ard rates Randy White of the Cowboys as the toughest. And the nastiest. And the . . . well, you get the idea.

When Ard, who played for the Giants from 1981-88, sensed White was breathing fire across the line of scrimmage, he knew a headache was likely to follow. What else could be expected of the fearsome defensive tackle who anchored the famed Dallas "Doomsday Defense" and came to be known as the "Manster." As in, half man, half monster.

"I put him in the Hall of Fame," Ard said with a laugh. "In the beginning of my career, Randy was in the prime of his career and he would try to rip my head off, break my jaw. Everything that is illegal now was legal back then. He would take his hands and shove 'em up your facemask, pound your head.

"Randy had this mentality, which probably made him so great, he's like a Rambo guy, it's me vs. the world. I never said a word to the guy, ever. Darryl Grant of the Redskins I used to play against, big hugs afterwards. David Galloway of the Cardinals, it was, 'Hey, how you doing?' You always talk to the guy you play against. With Randy, hell no."

About five years into his career, Ard noticed a definite change in the way White attacked him. No more head slaps, no more attempts at decapitation. Ard made mention of this one day in the offseason of 1987 when he attended a concert with his buddy, Brian Baldinger, an offensive lineman who played for the Cowboys.

"I said Randy was starting to mellow out, he'd actually been a pretty nice guy when we'd been on the field, he hadn't given me cheap shots in maybe a year," Ard said.

Bad move.

Dave Jennings (Photo courtesy of the New York Giants)

"Before our game against the Cowboys, Baldinger tells White, 'Ard said you've slowed down, you don't have it any more.' He just freaking takes the story and works it to death. So the first play of the game we run a sweep, and Randy was in his frog stance and he exploded off the ball and he was going to try to rip my head off, he didn't care about the play, he was going to rip my head off. I pull, and he explodes through into the backfield, lands and falls on his face. I didn't see it because I was pulling, but I heard it was very comical.

"The rest of the game he's trying to rip my freaking head off like he did when I was younger. I get off the field, I'm talking to Baldinger,

I said, 'Man, White was a dick today, a total dick.' Brian starts laughing and says, 'I told him you said he was old.' I said, 'You asshole.'"

Making 'Em Sweat

After kickoff, there was never any problem with Lawrence Taylor. Wind him up, watch him go. There were times before the game, though, when Taylor made everyone squirm.

"There was an ESPN Sunday night game against the Redskins at home when I made my teammates and coaches sweat," Taylor said. "For whatever reason, they had moved the game from eight o'clock to seven. It was on the itinerary, and I guess all week long, every day, the coaches went over it so there'd be no fuckup."

Game time was approaching and still no LT. Running back O.J. Anderson, for good luck, used to have Jim Fassel, an assistant to Ray Handley in 1991 and 1992, stretch his hamstrings during warm-ups. Fassel was stretching Anderson when he noticed that a certain Pro Bowl linebacker wasn't yet on the scene.

"So I ask O.J., 'Where's Lawrence?'" Fassel said. "O.J. said, 'He's running late, he'll be here, though.' Well, now it's getting later, and no LT. And O.J. tells me, 'I'm getting nervous too.' So about 20 minutes before kickoff, I walk in the locker room and see Lawrence sitting there tying his shoes. I said, 'Nice to see you here,' and he says, 'Well why didn't somebody tell us the damn game was moved to seven o'clock?'"

Bill and Phil

Ask Bill Parcells about Phil Simms and an unusual sentiment surfaces.

"Phillip, I love him," Parcells said. "I just think we both needed each other, that's one thing we both realized."

Need is a funny thing. Parcells became the Giants' head coach in 1983, and he certainly needed to find a franchise quarterback. Simms was a first-round draft pick in 1979, a small-town kid from Morehead State, and he certainly needed someone to believe in him. The two engaged in battles early in their relationship. Parcells believes he knows precisely when they bonded.

"There was a game against Kansas City in '84 that was probably the turning point for Phil and me," Parcells said, "in terms of he understood what I was trying to do and I gained a tremendous respect for what he was about."

This was heading into the final month of a breakthrough 1984 campaign, as Parcells was about to secure his first winning season and first playoff berth as a head coach. Along the way, he was breaking Simms in. In Week 13, the Giants and Simms were both struggling, trailing the Kansas City Chiefs 27-13, seemingly headed to a loss.

"There were about six or seven minutes to go," Parcells said. "We couldn't, really all day, get Phil to execute what we thought were good play selections. Kansas City had a couple of ball-hawking defensive backs named Albert Lewis and Deron Cherry, and Phil was tentative.

"It wasn't just me. [Offensive coordinator] Ron Erhardt and I were discussing this on the phone. 'Bill,' he says, 'he's just not pulling the trigger.' This is a dialogue for a quarter and a half. He will just not throw what's there, he will not take a chance, he's too conservative, he will not do what we're asking him to do. So we're gonna lose the game, it's obvious.

"So I brought him over to the sideline and I said to him, 'Now look, I'm gonna take full responsibility for what I'm about to say here. If you throw an interception it's gonna be my fault. I want you to do exactly what I tell you to do and don't deviate.' I said,

'We're gonna get in this certain formation, it was called eight slot out, and we're gonna call a 70 protection and I want you to throw it to Zeke [Mowatt].'

"He looked at me like he was incredulous and he said, 'Every time?' And I said, 'Yeah, every time.'

"Well the first play he hits Zeke for 12, next play he hits Zeke for 30, the next play he deviates and hits Bobby Johnson, the fourth play he deviates and hits Bobby Johnson for a touchdown. We hold 'em, we come back, he hits Zeke for three or four more passes, he throws for 176 yards in the last seven minutes and we beat Kansas City, 28-27. That was I think the moment when I knew he was my guy, because he did listen to me, and I was able to turn the light on for him."

Highlight Run

George Martin called himself "really a frustrated tight end playing defensive end." It's no wonder when the ball was in his vicinity, it didn't escape his grasp.

Always, it seemed, Martin ended up with the ball in his hands. His three interception returns for touchdowns remain a record for a Giants lineman, and he calls his 78-yard jaunt against John Elway and the Broncos in 1986 "truly my career highlight."

On November 23 that season, Martin knew facing the Broncos (in a preview of Super Bowl XXI two months later) was a stiff test. "There was still some question as to how good we really are, because we really hadn't tested ourselves against the better clubs," Martin said. "John Elway was, what else can you say, he's a Hall of Famer, and at that time he literally could walk on water."

The Giants won, 19-16. In the second quarter, with the Giants trailing 6-3, Denver was backed up on its own 22-yard line when

Martin sniffed out a screen pass to Sammy Winder and was able to get to his feet after a Broncos offensive lineman tried to cut him.

"I leaped over him, and just then I see the ball coming over my head," Martin said. "I bat the ball up in the air and it comes down right in my hands.

"No kidding, I can see there was nothing but real estate ahead of me, and there was no way I was going to get into the end zone. So my first thought was let me lateral the ball to someone who's faster than I am. That included my 10 teammates, 11 guys on the other team and five of the referees. I remember Lawrence Taylor was there, and just as I was running down the field, Elway got between me and Lawrence and I couldn't lateral him the ball, but I kept faking like I was gonna do it. Lawrence kept saying, 'Give me the ball, give me the ball!' as we're running down the field.

George Martin (Photo courtesy of the New York Giants)

"Elway tries to tackle me and I stiff-arm him and throw him off to the sideline. All of a sudden I get this escort from Mark Collins and Carl Banks, all these guys are blocking for me, I keep running and the whole time Lawrence doesn't throw a single block, he's saying, 'Give me the ball, give me the ball!' And I eventually get to the end zone, and who's the first guy to tackle me? Lawrence.

"My dad was in the stands, it was nice. I presented him with that ball, which he cherished until his death."

LT's Greatest Hits

When a player achieves immortal status at his position, and that position is linebacker, you can be sure there's been some heavy hitting going on. Any "Greatest Hits" collection compiled for Lawrence Taylor would surely include several volumes.

He has a few favorites, collisions that are memorable for their ferocity.

"I caught Stump Mitchell one time at the goal line and almost broke that son-of-a-bitch's back," Taylor said. "He tried to jump in sideways, and I hit him dead in the back, and it was like he was an accordion. You bend that way, but I bent him back the other way. It was solid.

"But the most solid hit I ever had . . . you know [John] Riggins was a mother, right? Especially on the goal line. Riggins doesn't say shit to me. I'm a rookie, he doesn't even talk to me, right? And he had never said anything to me and I never said anything to him.

"We played them the second game my first year, and Riggins came over the goal line, and I caught that son-of-a-bitch, I mean, head on. BAM! That son-of-a-bitch went straight to the ground. That's when he broke the ice. He stood up and said, 'Good hit, rookie.' "

Anyone who made a living delivering punishment could not avoid getting punished. Taylor was no exception.

"I got kneed in the head by John Riggins," he said. "It was one of those sweep plays they always ran. I caught Riggins in the backfield, and he caught me right square in the head and, I mean, just knocked the shit out of me. And I'm standing out there, and didn't know where the hell I was.

"I'm sitting in the middle of the field out there and Harry Carson called to me like, 'LT, get lined up!' I'm like, 'Where the fuck am I?' And Harry looked at me and called time-out. It was maybe 'til the third quarter that I realized what was going on. It seemed like I was dreaming the whole thing."

Listen, Don't Talk

Of all the defenses that viewed Phil Simms as a target to be destroyed, two groups left indelible imprints. The rivalries between the Giants and Redskins and Giants and Eagles left a trail of blood, sweat, and tears on the field and some welts and bruises on Simms' muscular body.

"Dexter Manley was tremendous," Simms said of the Washington defensive end. "He talked a lot when we played against them, which was always fun. He did the talking, and I did the listening, because I figured don't ever say anything to him because he was tough enough.

"Dropping back, I could actually hear him as he was trying to get to me, snorting like a bull. I can remember it as plain as day, him snorting as he was rushing against Brad Benson or whoever was trying to block him. He always had something to say, but it was always good. There was never profanity, it was always, 'Dang, finally you held on long enough.' Sometimes you'd just have to laugh. Late in the game against us if he didn't get a sack you could hear him, I'd be under center and he'd say, 'Hey, if he takes a knee will somebody let me touch him? Maybe they'll give me a sack.'"

As much as Simms can wax poetic about the Eagles' Reggie White—"I underestimated his greatness," he said—he saves his most eloquent praise for Jerome Brown, the Philadelphia defensive tackle whose career was cut short after five brilliant seasons when he was killed in a car accident prior to the 1992 season.

"The great, the late Jerome Brown, it's hard to say, probably was going to be a better player than Reggie White," Simms said. "He was Warren Sapp before Warren Sapp, as far as talking. He hated me, we played 'em twice a year, and all of a sudden he must have watched some film and, I don't know what it was, he couldn't hate me any more. He would hit me, sack me, pick me up and go, 'I love you man, you are unbelievable, you hang in there.' I know he meant it, too. Hey, it was one of the best things I ever had said to me on the field.

"You now what it told me? That means Jerome Brown and Reggie White and Clyde Simmons and Seth Joyner and all of 'em were sitting in their meetings and going, 'You know, we're gonna kill him, but there's something about this boy.' They must have been saying something good about me. That's pretty cool. That was the most wicked group. To think that I played 'em twice a year and still don't have something that's hurting me because of that. My God, it was unbelievable."

Old Yeller

The byplay and give and take between Bill Parcells and Lawrence Taylor was many things: Passionate, obscene, spirited, emotional, and laden with respect. The coach and linebacker squeezed the best out of each other, often only after some tense, testy, and titillating moments.

"He always used to stand directly to my left during the national anthem," Parcells said. "Nobody really noticed it. He was superstitious too, like me. He hated the Redskins, that was always a game I didn't have to really worry much about him, I would never really say too much to him because that was kind of a fierce rivalry, particularly if we were going down there.

"One day we were down there, and I hadn't said much to him. We were right there, the national anthem was just over, and he was standing right next to me. I turned, I don't know why I said this, I said, 'Are you gonna play today?' I just screamed at him, right in his facemask.

Lawrence Taylor (Photo courtesy of the New York Giants)

He came right back at me, he said, 'You just worry about those other son-of-a-bitches you're coaching.' He was almost spitting at me."

Trading Places

Phil McConkey could not have envisioned that the 1986 season would end in such personal glory: Scoring a touchdown in the Super Bowl to help the Giants to a championship.

McConkey, a receiver and punt returner, was jettisoned by the Giants during training camp that year and claimed off waivers by the Packers. After a month in Green Bay, McConkey was traded back to the Giants. The price tag was not staggering: A 1987 12th-round draft pick.

"I go to [Packers coach] Forrest Gregg's office, and he says, 'The phone's gonna ring, it's going to be Bill Parcells, we traded you back to the Giants, good luck,'" McConkey said. "The phone rings, it's Bill. He says to me, 'Those Packers drive a hard bargain.' I say, 'What are you talking about?' He says, 'I had to throw in a couple of clipboards with that blocking dummy to get you back.'"

McConkey was thrilled to be returning to the Giants. "Bill used to end every expression with 'my ass' this and 'my ass' that," McConkey said. "Players always thought it was better somewhere else. I figured out it wasn't. I said to him, 'Bill, the grass is greener, my ass.'

"He made me write it on the chalkboard in the locker room when I got back, it stayed up there the whole season. I saw Chuck Knox [former head coach of the Rams, Bills, and Seahawks] at a Super Bowl years later, and he was sitting down with a bunch of coaches, he called me over and said it was the greatest quote he'd ever heard from a player."

Bonus Money

The goal each and every week is clear: Win the game. But along the way, adding in a few incentives to spice up the proceedings doesn't hurt.

So it was early in the 1988 season, as the Giants were clinging to a 12-10 lead in Dallas, desperate to navigate toward a hard-earned victory, when Phil Simms suddenly came up with a brainstorm idea.

Why not sweeten the pot?

"I was taught all my life the quarterback is pretty vocal, were the order givers and all that stuff," Simms said. "We're trying to run the clock out, there's like five minutes to go, we're winning by two points and I go, 'Guys, if we run this clock out, I swear to you I'll bring $10,000 in cash to practice tomorrow, we'll throw it down in the room and fight for it.'

"Everybody is like, 'Yeah! Let's go!' Because they knew I'd do it. That's how desperate and how much I wanted it at the moment. Looking back, I go hell, that was probably who knows how much of my paycheck. But I would have done it. I remember it was unbelievable, the emotion, we pick up a first down, everybody was so into it. It wasn't the money, it was just everything. The words, the money, the bonding of athletes."

Seeing dollar signs dancing in their heads, the Giants must have been successful in playing keep-away from the Cowboys by running out the clock.

Yes?

"No we did not," Simms said. "We had a third and about a foot and we lost like a yard and had to punt it, we got it down to about a minute something, we ended up winning the game. I did bring in quite a bit of cash the next day and split it among all the offensive linemen. Actually I did bring in like two grand. Not $10,000, though."

The Tackle That Wasn't

The great play by the great player almost always includes a foil—someone to throw the pitch that gets knocked out of the park, or give up the game-winning goal, or miss the free throw that leads to the deciding basket. For every Don Larsen there's a Ralph Branca. In a career filled with breathtaking exploits, Randall Cunningham needed his Carl Banks.

"I laugh about it," Banks said, "because when I was with Randall I told him, 'Man, I made you famous, didn't I?' We always joke about that to this day. What else could I do?"

If Banks comes across as amiable in the face of adversity, that's because he understands his place in one of history's most incredible *Monday Night Football* moments. On the night of October 10, 1988, the Eagles defeated the Giants 24-13 in another clash of bitter division rivals. Bursting forth from the action was a single play by Cunningham that instantly grew into a highlight for the ages.

A highlight, that is, for the Eagles quarterback. Not so for Banks.

The play lives on in the memories of those who were at the Vet that night and remains etched in the minds of those who watched on television or care to re-create Cunningham's Houdini act via the eternal internet magic of YouTube.

It was early in the second quarter. The Eagles led 3-0 and were positioned on the Giants four-yard line when tight end Jimmie Giles faked a block on Banks and then ran into the end zone, eluding safety Terry Kinard. The ball never should have found its way to Giles, not with Banks deciphering the situation expertly and, at least for an instant, looking like the All-Pro linebacker he was.

Cunningham rolled to his right, faded back to the 10-yard line, and there was Banks, in hot pursuit, diving in like a torpedo seeking its intended target. Banks went for Cunningham's legs, driving him back to the 12-yard line, knocking the ever-so-elusive Cunningham off balance. The tackle should have stuck, but did not. Somehow, Cunningham was able to twist his body in mid-air and, while parallel to the ground, steadied himself by thrusting one hand onto the artificial turf. Cunningham, in a remarkable display of athletic grace, regained his footing, looked up the field, and fired an improbable touchdown pass to Giles.

After coming up empty on the tackle, Banks jerked his head around and saw Giles and the Eagles in joyous celebration. He threw himself to the turf, lying facedown in disgust before slowly getting to his knees and shaking his head in abject frustration.

"It was a rollout. I played my responsibility because when the ball faked I had to stay home in case the quarterback rolled out. I did and as he approached the line of scrimmage, I knew he was going to try to run," Banks said. "I went up to tackle him. I took his legs from under him. He caught himself with one arm—did basically a one-arm pushup—and threw a touchdown. I stood up, looked behind me and saw the tight end catch the ball and I just fell over in disbelief, like 'Holy crap!' "

The play did not define Banks, a sturdy, starting strong side linebacker on two Super Bowl championship teams with the Giants. The play, though, does live on as Banks' most famously missed opportunity.

"I once had a game against Randall where I had two or three sacks, but that was just one of those plays," Banks said. "I was a guy who didn't miss tackles. I never missed tackles; I took a lot of pride. We had a little chart—a missed tackle chart—and I didn't want to be on there for missing one single tackle. I knew how to tackle. I did what I did. At some point his ability took over and it was one of those deals, like you had your hand in Michael Jordan's face and he still hit the shot, you know? I gave it my best shot, he just made it happen for himself."

Thrill of the Chase

He was set to say goodbye, ready to end what easily translated into a Hall of Fame career. Lawrence Taylor, the great linebacker, determined that 1992 would be his last season with the Giants. But on November 8 of that season, Taylor tore his Achilles tendon chasing down Green Bay's Brett Favre. He was carted off the Giants Stadium field that day.

His plans were wrecked. Taylor knew he had to return, if only to walk away from the game, rather than be carried out, feeling helpless and defeated.

"You look at Dan Marino, Jerry Rice . . . you look at John Elway, you look at Jim Brown," Taylor said. "They want to dictate the way they go out. I've always remembered the story about athletes dying young. And I always said to myself, 'Yeah, that's the way I want to be.' I wanted to get out of the game while I was still remembered for the good things I could do on the football field.

"But I didn't want to go out like a sad sack. One of those what-have-you-done-for-me-lately guys. Just hanging on 'til the end, for a paycheck, for the ego, for the spotlight, for whatever reason. Kareem Abdul-Jabbar, for example, never should have hung around and played that last year."

Taylor returned for one more season, helping the Giants in 1993 make the playoffs in Dan Reeves' first year as head coach. Although he was plenty good, he was not the LT of old. He viewed himself as a superstar who grudgingly admitted his luster was fading.

"Let me tell you: It's a bitch when you lose the will to hit," Taylor said. "It's a bitch. Because you don't chase anymore. I used to chase, chase, chase, chase. You don't chase anymore; there's a pileup, you got four guys over there, and one of them son-of-a-bitches can bring him down, so I'll just stand back here and, you know, collect tickets. You look at yourself on the film and you see you're not hustling. And you're not sticking your head in there, and you're not doing the things that made you feared. You get tangled up with a guy you would have eaten alive when you were the real LT.

"And the worst thing in the world is to watch yourself on film, on that Monday, and the coach may say, 'Good job.' But you look at it and you sit there and you say to yourself, 'Now that's a damn shame,' because you know damn well you're not giving it everything you got. But what really hurts is when you know you're better than that but yet you're not willing to do anything about it. They're happy with it, fine. I never said that, 'If they're happy with it, it's fine.' I've always said, 'If I'm happy with it, it's fine.'"

New York State of Mind

Steve DeOssie, fresh out of the Roslindale suburb of Boston, spent the first five years of his NFL career with the Cowboys and never grew enamored with life in Texas. "The big myth about Dallas is they're great fans and knowledgeable football fans," DeOssie said. "The exact opposite is true. They're fair-weather fans and they really don't know their football. People will have you believe they invented football in Texas. Come to Giants Stadium, you're talking about people who know their football."

That's the admitted Northeast bias flowing from DeOssie, a part-time starter at linebacker for the Cowboys who eventually longed for a change of scenery. As a long-snapper, DeOssie would practice his craft prior to games and thus became a convenient pre-game target whenever the Giants were the opponent.

"I'm out there long-snapping, and you know how Bill Parcells likes to talk. He's out there talking to me, saying, 'I was one step away from grabbing you in the draft,'" DeOssie recalled. "He said

'I still might find a way to get you.' I wasn't thinking anything of it. For about three years we had that same conversation, it was, 'Hey Bill, how about getting me out of here?'"

This was not idle chatter. During a mini-camp prior to the 1989 season, Cowboys coach Jimmy Johnson summoned for DeOssie. "Steve, I'm afraid I got a little bad news for you," Johnson said. "I just got off the phone with Coach Parcells. I just traded you to the New York Giants."

DeOssie hasn't forgotten that moment. "There was silence for a few seconds and he goes, 'Well?'" DeOssie said. "I said, 'Well Coach, I'm waiting for the bad news.'"

The grass truly was greener for DeOssie, who blossomed with the Giants. He moved into the starting lineup, joining a menacing defense and an especially imposing linebacker corps.

"I got traded at the end of May and I was only with the team for about a month and a half before we go to training camp," DeOssie said. "What stuck with me and positively scared the life out of me was Bill Belichick and Bill Parcells having the faith in handing me the starting job and then making me the defensive signal caller. I'm looking around and I see Carl Banks over here and Pepper Johnson and Lawrence Taylor and I'm like that one thing that doesn't belong—that old *Sesame Street* song. I'm thinking to myself this is a tremendous leap of faith for these guys to assume: A, I belong on the field with these guys; and B, that these guys will actually listen to me in a huddle.

"Actually playing the game never frightened me, but that responsibility they gave to me, knowing how great that Giants defense was, when I sat back and thought about it, it scared the life out of me. They didn't give it to me for any other reason than because those guys didn't want to call the huddle. I was overwhelmed at one point with it. The fear of letting those guys down motivated me tremendously."

Rarely did DeOssie let his teammates down, as he emerged as a popular player in the locker room, with the media, and with Parcells and was a starter for a Super Bowl champion following the 1990 season.

DeOssie felt like he found a home after struggling along in Dallas.

"What amazed me about that team, having come from Dallas where there were a lot of, for lack of a better word, a good number of assholes on that team," he said. "My only exposure to the NFL was in Dallas where there was racism, there were guys who felt superior because of the money they made, all sorts of crazy crap going on in Dallas. I just thought that was what the NFL was like. I go to New York and I'm telling you, it was an asshole-free team. I couldn't believe it. We had one guy, Greg Cox, who was an asshole, but he was one of our better special teams players. Parcells got rid of him halfway through the [1989] season—found out he was not doing the right thing in the locker room.

"Then again, Maurice Carthon tells me five years after the fact that when I came in I was one of the first guys that kind of bridged the gap a little bit—the black-white thing. It didn't matter to me who I hung out with; I hung out with whoever was cool to hang out with."

The ties that bind him to the Giants grew stronger during the 2007 NFL Draft, when the Giants selected his son Zak, a linebacker from Brown University, in the fourth round. Of course, the proud papa was thrilled.

"If you look at him he's tall, he's lean, he's athletic, he's good-looking, he's smart," Steve DeOssie said, "and as I'm saying this I'm thinking I need a DNA test to justify all that child support payment I've had the last few years."

You Want Fries with That?

When Dan Reeves gets warmed up, y'all might as well set down a stool, kick up your heels, and take a load off. There's nothing like story time when Reeves cranks up that southern Georgia drawl to produce a homespun gem.

As the 1994 season progressed, there weren't many tall tales coming from Reeves. Not after the optimism of a three-game winning streak deteriorated into the misery of seven consecutive losses.

And so, as the struggling Giants limped into Houston to face the Oilers, they were desperate to end their losing ways.

Lo and behold, the Giants beat the Oilers 13-10 in an inelegant *Monday Night Football* game. For the win-starved Giants, though, it was a masterpiece and the first of what evolved into a season-closing six-game winning streak.

What happened after the coveted victory goes down in Reeves lore.

Three busses left the Astrodome carrying the Giants to the airport for the red-eye flight back to New Jersey. Reeves and his wife, Pam, rode in the lead bus, along with other team executives, including co-owner Wellington Mara and his wife, Ann. As soon as the bus pulled onto the highway, it was immediately stuck in traffic.

"We didn't go an inch in 20 minutes," Reeves said.

This was after 1 a.m., and Reeves and his coaches hadn't eaten anything since 4 p.m. when the team had its pregame meal. Hunger was rampant.

"At that time, you'll eat anything," Reeves said.

With the bus stopped dead in its tracks, Reeves noticed an open McDonald's about three-quarters of a mile away at the bottom of the next exit ramp. Spurred on by an empty stomach, Reeves, along

Dan Reeves (Photo courtesy of the New York Giants)

with team security official Mike Murphy, plus assistant coaches Mike Nolan, Pete Mangurian, and Earl Leggett, exited the bus and took off for fast-food relief.

Once inside, the Giants party ordered 24 hamburgers. The cooks began flipping burgers. Just then, Reeves glanced outside and noticed that traffic had started to move.

Reeves, nattily attired for the team charter flight, scurried outside and climbed the concrete wall of the highway underpass, attempting to flag down the bus. "There was this wino under the bridge," Reeves said. "He said, 'I ain't never seen nobody in a coat and tie here before.'"

Reeves was too late. The bus drove past him, leaving him stranded. The five men crammed their way into a cab, which happened to be waiting at the McDonald's drive-though window.

"We got to the airport and the buses were there," Reeves said. "But there were only two of them. They sent the other bus back to pick us up."

The bus sent back to find Reeves and Co. was Mara's.

Reeves groaned. "I said, 'Boys, this is probably the worst play I've ever called.'"

Unbeaten No More

There wasn't any evidence to predict what was about to happen. The Giants were 4-8 and wobbling down the stretch of the 1998 season as they braced to face the Denver Broncos at Giants Stadium.

It sure looked like a colossal mismatch. The Broncos rolled in with a record of 13-0 and were gaining momentum as a threat to match the Miami Dolphins' perfect 1972 season. Dating back to a year earlier, the defending-champion Broncos had won 18 consecutive games.

"I just remember just how big a game it was and probably playing one of my best games I've ever played," quarterback Kent Graham said.

As a decided underdog playing at home, the Giants upset the Broncos 20-16, but not without first encountering some harrowing moments. A 27-yard touchdown run by Terrell Davis put Denver ahead 16-13 with 4:08 remaining. Things looked glum when Gary

Brown (for the first time all season) fumbled the ball away, but the Giants defense stiffened, and Graham, with no time-outs, got the ball back on his own 14-yard line with just 1:49 left.

Graham needed to have one of those fantastic finishes made famous by John Elway, his counterpart on this day.

"You feel like you're going against Elway, the king of comebacks," Graham said. "It's like, 'Hey, can I do the same thing?'"

Graham, more lumbering than fleet afoot, took off and gained 23 yards to keep the desperation drive alive. The winning points came on Graham's 37-yard scoring pass to Amani Toomer with a mere 48 seconds to go. Graham finished up completing 21 of 33 passes for 265 yards and two touchdowns.

"I remember it being one of the biggest highlights of my career," said Graham, who spent five seasons with the Giants in two separate stints. "I was sitting out there, and when I threw that last touchdown, the fans just went crazy. What made it really special was my dad, Vic, was on the sideline for that game, about one of the only times he's been on the sidelines for a game. I came off to the sideline and he said, 'Well, Kent my boy, you did it. You guys got 'em.' I said, 'Dad, it's John Elway. You got to be kidding me. It's not over yet.' There was like 30 seconds left. He goes, 'I think it is.' And they didn't score."

Frankie Ferrari

There have been bigger Giants, certainly better Giants. But there has never been a member of the Giants quite like Frank Ferrara.

From his arrival in the summer of 1999 to his departure following the 2003 season, Ferrara was rarely on the field at defensive end but made his mark with a frenzied approach to training camp and practice. After just a few days around Ferrara, future

Hall of Fame defensive end Michael Strahan took a quick liking and dubbed him "Frankie Ferrari" because, you guessed it, of his nonstop motor.

Three times the Giants cut Ferrara, who was born in Brooklyn, raised in Staten Island, and spoke with the classic New YAWK accent that defined his roots.

Ferrara, who like his father—James Gandolfini's body double in *The Sopranos*—worked as a stunt man in the movies, notched his first NFL sack against the Cowboys on November 4, 2001, when he got around Pro Bowl guard Larry Allen and dropped Ryan Leaf. Of course, the achievement came with a story that only Ferrara could tell.

Ferrara did not expect to play and, battling hunger pangs, figured what would it hurt to grab a little halftime snack? He wolfed down a hot dog with mustard and sauerkraut, plus two chocolate chip cookies, and prepared to watch the second half from the sideline. But Ross Kolodziej, an emergency starter for injured Keith Hamilton, got hurt, and Ferrara was forced onto the field.

"I'm chasing Ryan Leaf and burping sauerkraut," said Ferrara.

Runner Walks Away

Players hang on. Not always, but almost. The money. The fame. The competition. The love of the game. These are strong, intoxicating lures that few can resist.

The vast majority of athletes are cast aside, released, cut, waived, informed that their services are no longer required. Their minds say they can still play, but their bodies betray them. They are too old, too slow, too worn. They are done. When no team will have them, they grudgingly admit that enough is enough, and then they retire.

Tiki Barber did not need to consider such finalities. There he was, doing his thing during the 2006 season, his 10th with the Giants, playing better than almost any other running back in the NFL, breaking records, leading his team and most of the league in rushing on a weekly basis, defying a time-tested axiom: Once a running back is on the back side of 30, his effectiveness inevitably is compromised, because no one outruns Father Time.

There were no signs on the field that Barber was nearing retirement, yet his decision to turn away from football and the Giants was shocking only to those who did not know him well.

"The bottom line," Barber explained, "is that I want to do what I want to do, which is walk away."

Barber announced in mid-October that the 2006 season would be his last. He was 31 years old and had two years remaining on a contract that would pay him nearly $9 million. His love of the game had waned, and his acceptance of the trappings of the game had expired. The grind of practice wore on his body and especially his mind. He felt less and less kinship with players who for the most part were younger and, in his mind, not as intellectually inquisitive as he. He lived in Manhattan, married with two young sons. Almost all of his Giants teammates opted for New Jersey condos near Giants Stadium.

His body, a chiseled 200-pound block, took such a beating during games that it took nearly an entire week to heal. By then, it was time to strap it on again for another round of punishment.

"After the Indy and Washington games I felt like death," he said early in his last season.

He feared not being able to romp with his sons because of arthritic joints, or, even worse, that his keen mind would be forever blunted by the debilitating after-affects of a concussion. A self-described "computer geek" from the University of Virginia,

Barber, during his football days, aggressively laid the groundwork for his second career in the media, and he was eager to get started with the next phase of his life.

"Nothing is guaranteed to you," Barber said. "Especially not sports. Now that I know I can guarantee how I'll be remembered as an athlete, as being at the top of my game, I think I would be foolish not to jump at that and move on to something else that I find exciting."

The idea of going out at the peak of his physical powers pleased him: Never, Barber insisted, would any fan of the Giants be able to say, "You should have seen him back in the day." Never, Barber maintained, would anyone ever accuse him of being just another guy.

Barber actually gave serious thought to retiring following the 2005 season, but he felt the Giants were on the verge of making a serious Super Bowl run, and he didn't want to leave the party before it got cooking. Alas, Barber miscalculated, as the Giants of 2006 labored to an 8-8 record and a first-round playoff ouster. Barber was typically brilliant with 1,662 rushing yards, but he could not be enticed to come back, despite pleas from fans to return. Some even called him selfish for leaving.

"There is something fundamentally wrong about that," Barber said. "Because as someone who has ownership over my own life, and has been given the God-given thing that all of us have, which is free will, I should be able to choose when I want to leave and if I want to stay."

Emotion was rarely part of the equation, as Barber never appeared melancholy about his decision or unnerved about leaving the game that catapulted him to fame and fortune. "I understand the sadness that comes with that—the loss that I'll feel," he said. "But I'm also excited about life and what's in front of me. That tempers some of the sadness that people may be looking for."

Barber did grow increasingly cranky as his final season unraveled around him. He openly criticized the offensive decision-making and ripped head coach Tom Coughlin with alarming regularity.

Teammates were almost unanimously supportive; most secretly envied Barber for the independence that allowed him to exit on his own terms.

"It's hard for people to accept because they look at it as: How could he give up such a great job, making all that money?" defensive end Michael Strahan said. "To be honest with you, sometimes this beating is not worth any money, any accolades, or anything else that somebody could give you."

Barber retired owning more than a dozen Giants records, departing as the greatest running back in franchise history. Four days after he scored a touchdown in the Pro Bowl, Barber was introduced by NBC as a correspondent for the *Today* show and an analyst for *Football Night in America*, a role he held until 2010. After a failed attempt at an NFL comeback in 2011, he is now a radio talk show host for the CBS Sports Radio Network.

The runner had indeed walked away.

Chapter 3

THE FOUNDERS

Thanks but No Thanks, Gov

The call came in the afternoon, during a mid-day meal.

"In those days you didn't have lunch," Wellington Mara explained, "you had dinner and you had supper."

This was back in the mid-1920s, the first years of existence for the New York Giants, when the Mara family, residing at 155th Street and Riverside Drive on the Upper West Side of Manhattan, was sharing a dinner table with close family friends, Al Smith, the governor of New York, and his wife.

Tim Mara, a legal bookmaker, had purchased the Giants in 1925 for $500 and was not receiving a strong return on that investment. On this day, the Maras were awaiting word on the outcome of a road game, word in the form of a call from the head coach, as no radio reports existed.

Finally, the phone rang and Tim Mara took the call. Not only had the Giants lost, but the attendance was meager, meaning the Giants' share of the gate receipts would not cover expenses for the team's return train trip. More money would have to be siphoned off the Maras' own savings to get their team home.

"We were all very disappointed," said Wellington Mara, who at the time was barely 10 years old and hearing the bad news along with his parents and older brother, Jack.

Just then, Smith—a few years away from running in 1928 for president of the United States—had a suggestion for his friend.

"Tim," Smith said, "get rid of it. It will never amount to anything."

Tim Mara understood the odds of turning a profit on this foray into football were not good, but he couldn't follow Smith's advice.

"My father said, 'The boys would never stand for that,'" Wellington Mara said. "I was there, it's a true story, I seen it done."

Of course, the team eventually made the entire Mara clan wealthy.

"Fortunately for the rest of us," said John Mara, Wellington's oldest son, "my father didn't take Al Smith's advice."

Money Matters

Sam Huff was drafted by the Giants in 1956 and emerged as an immediate star at middle linebacker. He won the NFL's defensive Rookie of the Year award and sparked a defense that led the Giants to a championship. There wasn't much more Huff could have accomplished.

What a bargain at a rookie salary of $7,500. Heading into his second year, Huff expected to receive a lucrative raise from team owner Wellington Mara.

"He offered me a $500 raise," Huff said. "I was Rookie of the Year! I said, 'You got to be kidding!'"

Huff played his second season for $8,000 and his third season for $9,000.

"That was awful, trying to negotiate with Wellington Mara," Huff said.

Established as one of the league's best players, Huff believed his time had come to make a financial killing. He headed to training camp one summer in Winooski, Vermont, without signing his contract, confident he could squeeze more money out of Mara.

"I go to his office, just he and I," Huff said. "He talks a little bit and he said, 'I want you to sign this contract.' I looked at it and I said, 'No, well, I can't sign it, it's not enough money.'

"He said, 'It's all you're gonna get.' I said, 'Well, Wellington, you're gonna force me to play out my option.'

"God, I said the wrong thing. The man, I had never seen him angry and let me tell you what, you don't want to see Wellington Mara angry. I made him angry. His face got bloodred. He stood up, he's not a big man, but he stood up and he grabbed every paper he could grab, books, whatever was on that desk, and he threw 'em down, papers flew seemed like everywhere. He said, 'I want to tell you something, you're gonna sign this contract, you're not gonna play out your option, you're a New York Giant, now sign this damn contract!'

"I said, 'Yes, sir.' I never wanted to make him angry again."

The Survey Says

Bob Lurtsema was a character. No two ways about it.

"This guy Lurtsema was not a serious individual," tight end Bob Tucker explained. "He was just a riot, one of the funnier guys on the team, kept everybody laughing. Dry humor. If you ever saw him, you'd start laughing right away."

Wellington Mara was not a character. No two ways about it.

Lurtsema, a slow-moving defensive end, had a four-year stay with the Giants, ending in 1971. There are those who believe Mara did not appreciate Lurtsemas antics and greased the skids for his departure.

"Bob Lurtsema was the player representative," Tucker said. "This was the time when the Players Association was in its infancy and trying to get a foothold as a union. The job of these player reps was to organize the team, there was a big to-do all around the league with any player rep who was making inroads, the team made sure they got the reps the hell out of there.

"Wellington Mara was on the Management Council, so when it came time to negotiate the deal with the union, Wellington was a little taken aback by his position. He wanted to know what the players thought of him, because now he's on the Management Council, essentially fighting against the players. He asked Lurtsema to give us this survey. Lurtsema went around and explained to everybody what he was doing, saying, 'Wellington wants to know what you think of him.'

"So Lurtsey takes this survey and gives it to the players. Some of the comments were, 'He's a jerk, he's a this, he's a that,' they really didn't mean it. If it were somebody else asking, you'd give a serious answer. With Lurtsey asking, you got some flip remark.

"The day after Wellington Mara called him into the office at Yankee Stadium, wanted the results of the survey and Lurtsey essentially told him all the flip remarks. Well, the very next day Lurtsey was traded to Minnesota, and we missed him."

The Lean Years

The Giants came tantalizingly close to winning the NFL title in 1963, losing the championship game to the Bears 14-10. That ended a three-year run in which the Giants participated in (and lost) three straight NFL championship games.

No one could have foreseen that a long, painful drought was about to dominate the Giants landscape.

The next time the Giants qualified for the playoffs was 1981. The 17 lean years included five head coaches, too many unqualified players, and countless hordes of disgruntled fans.

And one man who claims responsibility.

"It was very largely my doing," Wellington Mara said. "I made a lot of decisions. The Jets had started and I was defending our turf, I didn't want the Jets to take the play away from us, I wanted us to have a winning team, and I misjudged the ability of the core of our team, I thought they were better than they were. I thought by making a deal here or making a deal there, trading a draft choice or a young player for an established player, I could keep us going.

"The result was I brought in guys who were all right, but we sacrificed our future. When you start making mistakes, it's just like making good decisions, they multiply."

Wellington Mara ran the football side of the operation while his older brother, Jack, handled the business side. Jack died in 1965, and Wellington shouldered a dual role. "Now I was the whole wheel," he said.

Seeking continuity and hoping to stabilize the team on the field, Mara signed Allie Sherman to a long-term contract, sticking with him through the 1968 season.

"That period in the '70s really wore on him, he really hurt, because he wanted to win so badly," said John Mara, Wellington's oldest son. "I think part of the problem we had back then was he was too loyal to many of his former players, put them in positions of responsibility, and as a result we had some poor drafts. He hung with the coaches a long time, that definitely came back to haunt us."

Wellington Mara also second-guesses his reluctance to come clean with the paying customers.

"Another thing was I also misjudged the loyalty of our fans," he said. "Even though we had rotten teams, we didn't lose any customers. They would certainly have understood if I had said, 'Look, we'll clean out the old, build this team with the draft, and in three or four years we'll be back up there. Will you guys stay with us for those three or four years?' The answer would have been a resounding yes, but I misjudged that."

Frank-ly Speaking

He was back on the West Coast trying to finish up his degree at USC and Frank Gifford figured he'd had enough of the New York Giants and pro football. As a first-round pick in 1952, Gifford served as an insurance policy in case Kyle Rote's legs gave out and, in his mind, spent too much time on defense as a two-way player.

Gifford was about ready to quit.

"At the end of 1953 we went 3-9, and I didn't come out of the last seven games, I was making $8,000 a year, and I was making twice that much working in the movie studios in California," Gifford said. "Pro football wasn't that big a deal, and we were getting killed playing in the Polo Grounds. I just said the hell with it."

One phone call changed Gifford's thinking and paved the way for a Hall of Fame career. Team owner Wellington Mara called Gifford, pleaded with him to return and promised changes, among them Jim Lee Howell replacing Steve Owen as head coach.

"Without Wellington Mara I would have never come back," Gifford said. "I had no one else to talk to. He's the only reason I stuck around. He brought in [Vince] Lombardi under Jim Lee Howell, who was more of a caretaker than anything else. Lombardi coached the offense and [Tom] Landry coached the defense, and three years later we went from what was basically the bottom, as far as you could go, to winning the NFL championship.

Frank Gifford (Photo courtesy of the New York Giants)

In This Corner . . .

It is impossible to play the role of referee when two sides can't even agree what time the game begins. That's the situation Giants public relations director Ed Croke found himself in as he tried to appease team owners Wellington Mara and his nephew Tim, warring factions that split a family and a team in two.

"Wellington had his press conferences, Timmy had his, and I ran both of 'em," Croke said. "Wellington said he wanted to run a press conference, we went down to the press room, Timmy would find out about it and say, 'What time is his?' I'd say, 'Noon,' and he'd say 'I want one at two o'clock.' It's 50-50 ownership, you work for both of 'em."

The terrible infighting made the losing of the '70s all the more grating.

"It's a sad thing when Irish fight, they're the worst people in the world to get in a fight with," Croke said. "The Italians have their vendettas, but when Irish disagree it's like for life. It got down to stuff like, I did all the advance road work, you go to an out-of-town hotel, the both of 'em are going to show up, the old days you put them in suites next to each other. Now I have to spend an hour with hotel people, saying, 'OK, Wellington Mara is going to be on the 18th floor of the southwest corner of the hotel, and put Timmy as far away from him, on the first floor of the south tower. Don't even get them in the same elevators.'

"Then I made a mistake, both of 'em wanted limousines on game days to take their families, I used to order limos from the same company. Until one day one of 'em went down and said, 'How come there are two limos here? I need one and cancel the other one.' The second Mara comes out, there's no limo, who they gonna blame, they call me and say, 'Where the fuck's the limo?' So from then on I used to use two different limo companies on the road so there wouldn't be any conflict of which limo was which."

Coaching Search

The team was in turmoil. The Giants did not have a general manager. They did not have a coach. The owners, Wellington Mara and his nephew, Tim, were embroiled in a squabble nearly Shakespearean in its entanglements. They couldn't agree on a general manager and, amid the chaos, following the 1978 season Wellington Mara decided he'd better start looking for a new coach.

"We were getting nervous, it was getting later in the year and we needed to have a coach on board," said John Mara, in law school at the time and one of the Giants directors. "At the time my father had a conversation with John Madden, who was only recently retired from the Raiders. We thought Madden was interested for a while and then for whatever reason he decided against it.

"We also spoke to Joe Paterno back then. In fact, Paterno would later say that was one of his greatest regrets, that he never got to be the head coach of the New York Giants, because he had grown up in Brooklyn. We also brought in Dan Reeves. My father had Dan Reeves fly in, Tim found out we were bringing him in and contacted him and said, 'This is a 50-50 ownership situation, and I don't want you here.' That was enough to scare Dan off."

Finally, the Giants hired George Young as their general manager and Young hired Ray Perkins as head coach.

Family Feud

As the story goes, the Giants were in such disarray following the 1978 season that NFL commissioner Pete Rozelle—attempting to settle bitter family infighting between owners Wellington Mara and his nephew, Tim—insisted the team hire George Young as its general manager. That story is only partially true.

Andy Robustelli left as general manager and the process of naming his successor turned into a nasty public battle, with both Wellington and Tim insisting HE would pick the next GM.

"We started out no matter who we nominated, Tim rejected him and vice versa," said John Mara, Wellington's oldest son. "As a matter of fact, Pete Rozelle got involved and had us in separate rooms at one point. We'd each submit a list of candidates and he'd try to see if there were any common names on the list."

The name of Jan Van Duser appeared on both lists and he was offered the job. Van Duser, who worked in the NFL office, turned the Giants down.

"To be fair, George [Young] did not appear on either of the first lists that were submitted," John Mara said.

Young, who helped build the Colts and Dolphins, received the endorsements of former Giants Tom Scott and Frank Gifford, as well as Bobby Beathard, and Wellington was sold.

"At that point we realized anybody we recommended Tim was going to automatically reject," John Mara said, "so my father called Pete Rozelle and suggested HE recommend George, so in fact he did that. Tim then went to his friend, Frank Gifford, did some research, agreed, and that's how George came to be the general manager."

By George

In 33 years in the NFL and 19 as the general manager of the Giants, George Young left a legacy as an absolute original.

Young, who died on December 8, 2001, at the age of 71, was named the league's Executive of the Year an unprecedented five times and built the Giants two Super Bowl championship teams. He also gave Bill Parcells his first head-coaching job, drafted Lawrence Taylor, took a first-round gamble on a kid from Morehead State named Phil Simms, and uttered what may be the most accurate portrayal of big-time professional sports in the modern era when he said, "Any time they say it's not about the money, it's always about the money."

He could be incredibly stoic, so much so that Ernie Accorsi, a close friend for 31 years and his successor as the general manager, once asked Young how he remained so outwardly unaffected during close games.

"He wouldn't make a peep," Accorsi marveled. "I asked him one time, 'How do you do that?' He said, 'If I said anything, would it make a difference?'"

Upwards of 300 pounds before losing more than 100 pounds later in life, Young often patted his perspiring brow while getting worked up and flailed his arms as if he were trying to imitate an enormous helicopter attempting to rise from the earth. He didn't like it when fans would spot his rotund physique on the sideline during training camp and shout, "Give 'em the money, George!" when one player or another was holding out in a contract dispute. That didn't stop Young from regularly engaging fans in discussions or answering their letters with hand-written responses.

"He'd label people quite often and often the labels were pretty accurate," said John Mara, the Giants' executive vice president and son of owner Wellington Mara. "So-and-so was 'a runaway freight train,' describing an employee in the office, So-and-so was 'a lifestyles guy,' So-and-so was 'a silver spooner.' I think he referred to me several times as 'a silver spooner.'"

Once, when a Giants player was arrested outside a nightclub for soliciting a prostitute, John Mara asked Young, incredulously, "What the hell is the matter with this guy?" Young's response? "John, a man with an erection does not always think rationally."

George Young had a way with words.

"I remember asking him about a former assistant coach who had gotten dismissed from another position," Mara said. "I said, 'This guy's available now, do you think we'd be interested?' George says, 'He has some health problems, John.' I said, 'What do you mean?' He said, 'It's called pork disease. He porks everything in sight.'"

Phil Who?

A first-round draft pick is a general manager's legacy, and in 1979 the downtrodden Giants turned their desperate eyes to George Young, recently hired to lift the team out of despair.

The Giants owned the No. 7 overall pick and they most assuredly were in the market for a quarterback. Young's first significant move running the Giants was a monumental surprise: The selection of Phil Simms out of the small-school Morehead State program. At the Marriott Marquis in Manhattan, the site of the NFL Draft, Giants fans hooted and jeered, disgusted with the choice.

"Most people at that time in '79 wanted us to pick Jack Thompson of Washington, the Throwin' Samoan," John Mara said. "He certainly had the bigger reputation. I remember asking George before the draft about that and he told me about this blond quarterback from Morehead State, and I said, 'George, but Jack Thompson, the Throwin' Samoan.'

"He put his glasses down at the end of his nose, looked over his glasses at me and said, 'John, you're paying me a lot of money to be the general manager to make these decisions. Just trust me on this one.'

"It was very gutsy pick, a kid from Morehead State, absolutely. I remember when we picked him, cringing, as people at the draft booed him. I didn't know anything about him, then when I saw his haircut I said, 'My God, this is the guy?' He had that real Prince Valiant look. Little did I know."

Tearful Goodbye

He could have done something. Could have prevented what was going down. As the co-owner of the team, Wellington Mara had the authority, had the power to say no.

And yet, he did not. Mara kept silent, unable to control his emotions, sitting in the back of a jam-packed press conference and openly weeping on that June day in 1994, when Phil Simms was officially released. It was a bitter end to a brilliant career for Simms, and Mara was sickened as the sad episode unfolded.

"It just welled up in me, I just couldn't keep it in that day at the press conference," Mara said.

Following the 1993 season, Simms was viewed as a physical risk coming off a shoulder injury. General manager George Young, torn between his feelings for Simms and, with the advent of the salary cap era in the NFL, worried about the financial ramifications of keeping an aging, hurting star, decided that the team could not afford to wait to learn whether Simms would be healthy by the summer. Much to Mara's dismay, Young decided to cut Simms loose.

"I thought George, in his zeal to save the team some money, he had let Simms go before his usefulness had disappeared," Mara said. "I made a special trip over to New York to our doctor, Russ Warren, this was in early spring, to get the doctor's best opinion on what were Phil's chances of regaining his effectiveness. I came away completely convinced by the middle of July, Phil would be as strong as ever. And despite that, George felt in the best interest of the team he would go in a different direction.

"I had the power to stop that, to veto that, but I just thought we've given this guy this job, it's his responsibility, I don't think I should impose my judgment on his. I had a very strong personal distaste for that deal. I felt Simms had done so much for the team and I had great confidence in him, I thought he could do it again. I know it came as a great shock to Phil, too. Actually it probably paved his way for a great career in broadcasting, but at he time he was very unhappy about it."

Simms had a brief flirtation with the Browns but, ultimately, never played again.

"Part of me wanted him to play someplace and be a big star," Mara said, "but the other part, I was glad that he retired as a Giant."

Football 101

The day before the Giants in early 1991 were set to face the Bills in Super Bowl XXV in Tampa, John Mara paid a visit to the Florida hotel room occupied by Preston Robert Tisch. Mara, armed with a law degree and clout as the oldest son of Giants owner Wellington Mara, was there to nail down negotiations with Tisch, who was poised to purchase half of the franchise.

"I wasn't sure we had a deal until I left the hotel room that day," John Mara said. "After concluding the deal he asked me who were the teams in our division, and I said, 'Man, this guy just spent all that money.' I thought it was amazing he didn't know that. His football knowledge since that time has obviously increased many times over."

Tisch, who preferred to simply be called Bob, was co-chairman of the Loews Corporation and one of the country's wealthiest and most philanthropic individuals. He spent $75 million to purchase a 50 percent interest in the Giants and, hardly qualified as a football expert.

"Early on before he got to know a lot of the players, he would walk through the locker room, he'd have a politician, he once had Mayor Dinkins in there, walking from locker to locker to introduce him to some of the players," Mara said. "Some of the players who he didn't know caught on to the fact that he didn't know them and they would switch lockers. He would generally go to a locker, look up at the nameplate and he would introduce Mayor Dinkins to the wrong guy."

Football was not Tisch's specialty. Finance was.

"I was also amazed how quickly he understood and learned what our business was about," Mara said. "What our shortcomings and strengths were as a business and that he could come to some of those conclusions so quickly."

He passed away on November 15, 2005, at the age of 79.

Master of Impersonation

He can't prove it, but tight end Bob Tucker believes—as did many of his teammates—that star defensive end Fred Dryer was traded away because of a seemingly harmless joke during training camp in 1972.

"We used to have the rookie shows every year in training camp, we used to have a lot of fun, roasting players and coaches, owners or whatever," Tucker said. "Freddie Dryer wasn't a rookie, but he did a little skit on Wellington Mara, and Freddie was let go the next year, traded to Los Angeles, this was a great defensive end. I don't think Wellington appreciated his effort, that it belittled him."

After football, Dryer went on to enjoy a successful acting career—most notably as the star of the *Hunter* TV series. "Freddie did an excellent imitation with the mannerisms and the speech and it was a riot," Tucker said. "Freddie was let go, and we couldn't believe it. I can't say for certain that was the reason why, but that was certainly the feeling."

A Chair-Razing Experience

Wellington Mara was famous for his Mount Rushmore expression during games, his stoic, can't-tell-if-he's-winning-or-losing countenance. Animated, he was not.

Human, however, he was.

"We're playing the Redskins at RFK Stadium, and where we used to sit there was a little auxiliary photography booth at the very, very top of RFK," said John Mara, Wellington's son. "It required you to climb up through the upper stands and up all these stairs, it was quite a long haul to get up there.

"We're playing them in a Monday night game under Bill Parcells in the early '80s, and we went for it on a fourth down and came up short, they stopped us. We were sitting on these little wooden folding chairs and I had never seen him lose his temper quite this badly. He got up and he stomped his foot on this chair and kept stomping on it until it was just broken into pieces.

"I finally looked at him and said, 'You got it, Dad, I think you got it, it's gone, there's nothing left.' He will on occasion lose his temper, but he's usually very controlled, particularly during games. I just was so startled with that."

Hole in One

Wellington Mara prided himself on remaining calm during games. He did, however, admit to a momentary lapse.

"We had a game in St. Louis, we didn't have a very good team, and Brad Van Pelt, who was our star, had a pulled groin," Mara said. "Bill Belichick was our special teams coach, a very fine coach, but at that time he had tunnel vision. Van Pelt couldn't play in the game, we had a two-touchdown lead in the closing minutes of the game, the Cardinals line up to kick off, I look up and there's Van Pelt on the kickoff return team, hadn't played the whole game.

"They kick off and Van Pelt re-injures his groin. That drove me up the wall. I kicked a hole in the wall of the booth I was in. Then I wrote a letter to Billy Bidwill the next day, asked him to send me a bill for the damages. Went back there the next year, the hole was still there."

Bill Parcells (Photo courtesy of the New York Giants)

Penny for Your Thoughts

Bill Parcells got his head-coaching start in 1983, left the Giants following the 1990 season with two Super Bowl victories, moved on to the Patriots, then the Jets, and finally to the Cowboys, but he never completely allowed all the Giants blue to escape from his veins.

Wellington Mara is part of the reason why.

"He was always there for me," Parcells said. "I would regard him as a good friend."

The two shared a playful tradition, even after Parcells bolted and hooked on in Dallas, housed in the same NFC East division as the Giants.

"We kid each other back and forth occasionally," Parcells said. "He knows I'm superstitious, and he's a little superstitious himself, I might add. He knew I would not pick up pennies with the tails up. Quite frequently before each season that I coached, even when I was gone from the Giants, he would send me a little note with a penny, heads up, attached to the note, which is really a good luck symbol. This year [2003], being that we were in the division now, it's a little different, he wrote, 'Good luck, up to a point,' which was I thought really cute. And there was a penny. It was great."

Stripped of Rank

The only interruption in Wellington Mara's 80-year career shepherding his beloved Giants came when he served in the navy during World War II. For more than three years, Mara saw action in both the Atlantic and Pacific theaters aboard aircraft carriers, emerging as a lieutenant commander.

With that service history on his resume, it was a natural that when a gritty, undersized receiver named Phil McConkey in 1983 arrived on the Giants doorstep, a bundle of energy from the Naval Academy, Mara took special notice.

McConkey took leave from the Naval Academy to attend that summer's training camp and beat the odds by making the team the next year. Mara, well versed in the names of not only the starters but the fringe players as well, never referred to McConkey by name when he greeted him.

"He'd call me lieutenant," McConkey said.

When McConkey stuck on the roster in 1984, he was surprised to hear that Mara had changed his pet designation for him. "He promotes me to commander," McConkey said. "In '83 I'm up to captain. We get in the playoffs, I keep getting these promotions, we win the Super Bowl and he's calling me admiral."

It was quite a rise through the ranks for McConkey. His demotion was shockingly swift.

"In 1987 we went on strike, we came back from the strike, and I got knocked back down to commander," McConkey said, "and it was a slow process to get any promotions after that."

Strike Out

The Giants were united and determined that they were not going to play. Labor unrest was rampant when on September 13, 1975, the team was set to boycott its preseason game against the Dolphins in Miami.

As defensive end George Martin remembers the situation, "We had some early labor disputes back then. We were going to boycott the preseason game against the Dolphins. We'd flown down there, it was obviously a televised game, and we were gonna boycott the game. It was a power play, an impromptu strike."

Hours before kickoff, the Dolphins caught wind of what the Giants were planning and were neither amused nor sympathetic.

"Don Shula and Bob Griese come into our locker room and they said what a shame this is, you guys are really disappointing our fans and boy, we just lit into them and ripped them a new one." Martin said. "We said, 'Get the hell out of here, this is our locker room!' We were pretty adamant. We were going back and forth, should we boycott? The vote was taken, and we were going to boycott the game."

Just then, into a room filled with militant intentions, strode a visitor.

"Wellington Mara walks in, no escort, by himself, right into the locker room, and when he walked in through that door you could hear hearts beating," Martin said. "Everybody gathered around, and Wellington Mara, who's a soft-spoken guy, didn't raise his voice.

"He says, 'Gentlemen, if this game is not played, and if it's not played on time, I will personally see that none of you ever play professional football in the National Football League again.' And he turned around and walked out."

What happened next would be telling. Would the Giants reject Mara's threat? Would they stand together and go forward with their strike?

"It was like the Three Stooges," Martin said. "You should have seen how people were getting dressed, fighting over different helmets, socks. That's the kind of power he wielded and the respect we had for him. Needless to say the game started a little bit late but we definitely played the game. That was the end of the boycott. We got the heck beat out of us [the Dolphins won 31-13], but the game went on."

Say It Ain't Joe

Joe Willie Namath, a New York Giant? Broadway Joe? It could have happened.

It almost happened.

It didn't happen.

Thank—or blame—Wellington Mara's steadfast integrity for that.

The Giants, coming off a 2-10-2 season, owned the first pick in the 1965 NFL Draft.

"We could have had Joe Namath," said Allie Sherman, the Giants head coach. "I wanted to coach Joe Namath very badly. I loved Namath. All our scouts were on board. And when the doctors checked him out, gave him a clean bill of health, we were all in agreement: We were going to take Joe Namath with our No. 1 pick. We'd have our franchise quarterback, the guy we could build on for the next 12 to 14 years, my new [Y.A.] Tittle."

What do they say about the best-laid plans?

"A couple of days before the draft, I walked into the office," Sherman said. "Well [Wellington Mara] was white as a ghost. He said, 'We have a problem.' "

Mara's league sources informed him that the Houston Oilers were going to take Namath with the first pick in the AFL Draft and Mara was sure that Bud Adams, the Oilers' deep-pocketed owner, would obliterate any Giants offer.

Sherman recalls Mara saying, "You know, Allie, we don't have that kind of money. He could just blow us out of the water with an offer. And then we don't have Namath, and we don't have a pick."

Sadly, Sherman saw Namath slipping away.

"It killed me to admit it, but Well was right," Sherman said. "We couldn't chance that."

The decision was made: The Giants would make Tucker Frederickson, a running back from Auburn, the first pick in the NFL Draft. As was the custom back then, Mara a few days before the draft wired the move into Pete Rozelle's office, as the commissioner wanted to know in advance who the top pick would be.

Seemingly, that was that.

"Until the next day," Sherman said, "when Well walked in the office, looking even paler than the day before, saying, 'You're not going to believe this.'

Jets owner Sonny Werblin, a consummate showman with a flair for the dramatic, obtained the rights to Namath from the Oilers and was set to bring the Alabama quarterback to New York's AFL team. Sherman was ecstatic.

"Well," Sherman reasoned, "Sonny isn't rich like Adams. He's a smart businessman, he knows people, he'll get Namath into TV and movies and shows and books and commercials. But we know all the same people he knows. We can do the same thing for him. And we're the Giants. We're the NFL. We have to take him now."

The Giants were getting closer to landing Namath. Until . . .

Mara shook his head.

Sherman still winces at Mara's response.

"I can't," Sherman recalls Mara saying. "I already called Pete. I already gave my word."

There was no argument from the head coach.

"That was it," Sherman said. "That's where it ended. The kind of man Well Mara has always been, he couldn't go back on his commitment. Now, Pete would have understood. In fact, in some ways, I'm sure Pete would have insisted, if he knew we'd changed our mind."

Mara's take is a bit different. He says the Giants did not have an opportunity to go back and get Namath after first committing to Frederickson. Mara does recall once the Jets got Namath's rights, he placed a call to the Cardinals (who owned Namath's NFL rights) to try to pry the rights away. Nothing materialized.

The Jets paid Namath $430,000, an outrageous figure in 1965. The Giants paid Frederickson $125,000. In the first game of his second season, Frederickson tore up a knee and was never the same.

"Maybe Tucker could have panned out if he hadn't blown out his knee," Sherman said. "It doesn't matter. If you ask people today who had the better career, Namath or Tucker, what do you think they'll say?"

Getting His Manning

Not obsessed. That was the vehement denial from general manager Ernie Accorsi. Not obsessed with procuring Eli Manning in the 2004 NFL Draft. Not obsessed with carving out his legacy by securing a franchise quarterback for the ages.

Forget about the words. Follow the actions. Accorsi went after Manning, the Mississippi quarterback, the way Ahab sailed the seas in search of the great white whale. Ahab was consumed by his obsession. Accorsi got his Manning.

"Ernie and I have talked about little else," said John Mara, the Giants executive vice president, after the deal was done, "for the last I don't know how many months."

Twenty-one years earlier, Accorsi, as the general manager of the Baltimore Colts, drafted John Elway with the first pick in the 1983 draft, convinced (as was everyone else) that this was a once-in-a-lifetime talent. The move was made even though Elway promised he'd never play in Baltimore and threatened to take his skills to minor league baseball.

"I was not about to go down in history as the guy who didn't pick him, I can tell you that," Accorsi said.

Less than a week later, Colts owner Robert Irsay traded Elway's draft rights to the Broncos. A stunned and disgusted Accorsi learned of the deal while watching an NBA playoff game on television. He resigned one year later.

Accorsi moved on to direct Cleveland's football operations and watched Elway thrust the knife and twist, repeatedly inflicting on the Browns' galling playoff losses. Clearly, Accorsi was haunted by Elway and what might have been.

A student of history, Accorsi learned through glory and agony the value of marquee quarterbacks. His NFL career began in Baltimore with Johnny Unitas on the scene. With the Browns, he traded for Bernie Kosar. With the Giants, he took a gamble on Kerry Collins when the Giants were shooting blanks finding a worthy successor to Phil Simms.

The Giants, by virtue of their 4-12 record in 2003, commanded the fourth overall selection in the 2004 draft and Accorsi knew what he must do. He was close enough to get Manning, a product of quarterback royalty, son of Archie and younger brother of Peyton. As a prospect, Accorsi considered Manning on par with Elway and Dan Marino. He was robbed of enjoying Elway. He wasn't going to get burned again.

"I think the only thing that parallels a quarterback is the great, great basketball players like Bill Russell and Michael Jordan," Accorsi said. "The history of this game tells us that they are difference-makers."

The San Diego Chargers owned the first pick and were set to take Manning, but fortune smiled on the Giants. The Manning family, dad Archie and son Eli, made it unequivocally clear that they would not play for the Chargers, fearful of what happened to Archie (11 years of losing in New Orleans) would befall Eli. After much maneuvering, plotting, and sweating, a draft-day trade was engineered.

Eli Manning was indeed chosen first by the Chargers. The Giants at No. 4 took Philip Rivers, a quarterback from North Carolina State, purposely as a lure, knowing San Diego's affinity for Rivers. The teams agreed to swap the rights to their selections, with the Giants also giving up a third-round draft pick in 2004 and first- and fifth-round picks in 2005. The price was steep, but Accorsi never blinked. A new era, with Tom Coughlin as head coach and Eli Manning as the face of the franchise, was about to be ushered in.

"It's not an obsession," Accorsi insisted. "I'm obsessed with the business. I know this, [former Dodgers and Padres executive]

Eli Manning (AP Images)

Buzzie Bavasi once said, 'I got weak knees twice in my life, when I walked into the Sistine Chapel and when I saw Sandy Koufax pitch.' When I see a player that I believe that strongly in, I'm going to do everything I can to get him. I'm just that way. I think it's a once-in-a-generation opportunity to get somebody you feel that strongly about."

The Son Also Rises

It was as if the father passed on the legacy to his son on a cool afternoon in the heart of Manhattan, where John Mara presented a eulogy for the ages in memory of his beloved dad, Wellington, the patriarch of the Giants.

In death, Wellington Mara was remembered as a man of great passion for his faith, his family, and his football team. In life, John Mara received a dignified and—considering the surroundings— extremely rare round of applause after lovingly eulogizing his father in front of more than 2,200 people inside St. Patrick's Cathedral. On this day, October 29, 2005, the 50-year-old John Mara showed everyone who did not already know that he in every way was his father's oldest son.

"He was the finest man we've ever known and will ever hope to know, and he was our dad," John Mara said, speaking for himself and his 10 sisters and brothers.

Mara, in a moving tribute, mixed humor with poignant remembrances of his father's rich life. He recalled when his mother, Ann, asked Wellington on their 50th wedding anniversary to renew their vows. "He was very reluctant at first," John remembered. " 'The original ones haven't expired yet,' he said."

He spoke of his father's traditional sideline practice attire: "That old floppy hat" and "that ridiculous stool" and his father's wardrobe— "usually wearing a shirt or jacket that was almost as old as he was."

He knew his dad would not have embraced the hubbub surrounding this grand funeral. "He would be so embarrassed by this," John said. "The police escort, the traffic being stopped, the bagpipes, and everything else, he would have just shook his head and tried to hide somewhere in the corner."

John brought tears to the eyes of the mourners when he recounted one of his final whispered conversations with his father.

John Mara (Photo courtsey of Charles Wenzelberg/NY Post)

"He smiled and said, 'I'll be there when you get there,'" John said. "It was his way of telling us that he was going to be OK, he was going to a better place."

Finally, after 15 minutes of emotional tug-of-war, John concluded with words from *Hamlet*: "Good night, sweet prince. May flights of angels sing thee to thy rest!"

As the recessional hymn, "On Eagles Wings," sounded, John lowered his head and returned to his seat. John had always resembled Wellington. On this day, the world learned how similar he actually was.

"His son gave one of the greatest speeches I have ever heard," said Mark Bavaro, the tough-as-nails tight end on two Super Bowl-winning Giants teams. "I don't know how he kept talking. We were all breaking down. It just shows—he's the son of a legend."

Fond Farewells

The Giants of 2005 evolved into a team good enough to go 11-5 in the regular season and capture first place in the NFC East, but devolved into a team bad enough to fail to score a single point in a dreadful 23-0 first-round playoff loss to the Panthers. Great the Giants were not. But no one could ever accuse them of not rising to the occasion when it came to bidding a proper and meaningful adieu to their respected owners.

Exactly three weeks apart, co-owners Wellington Mara and Bob Tisch passed away after battles with cancer, creating ruptures in a season that the franchise somehow managed to suture together. Sadness was the norm, but the Giants found a way to bring closure and pride to their First Families.

Prior to the October 23 game against the Broncos, head coach Tom Coughlin decided to tell the team about Mara's failing health, imploring the Giants to put a smile on the faces of both Mara and Tisch. The Giants beat the Broncos 24-23 with two fourth-quarter touchdowns.

A week later, Coughlin navigated the Giants through an emotional and draining gauntlet. Mara died on a Tuesday at the age of 89, and Coughlin had to get through his own personal grief, change his team's schedule to incorporate a Friday funeral at St. Patrick's Cathedral, and find a way to concentrate on football. Two days later, the Giants came as close as possible to producing a perfect game, trouncing their archrivals, the Redskins, 36-0 in front of a nearly-overwrought Giants Stadium crowd.

"He did a great job of making sure we didn't let the week's events distract us," running back Tiki Barber said of Coughlin. "And it didn't, obviously."

Obviously. Barber made sure the Giants emerged victorious. On the very first play from scrimmage, he raced down the left sideline for 57 yards, and the fans were roaring. By halftime, Barber had rushed for 171 yards en route to what was then a career-high 206-yard outburst.

Earlier in the week, Barber had been summoned to Mara's bedside to say a personal goodbye. Mara died the next day.

"I thanked him; to be able to have my best day on this day was something that I'll never forget," Barber said. "Sometimes history writes itself before it happens and I think we couldn't have written it any better than we did today."

The Giants amassed 262 rushing yards.

"If he said it once, he said it a hundred times: 'Run the ball, run the ball, run the ball,'" John Mara, Wellington Mara's oldest child, said of his father's football philosophy. "That was always his mantra when he came to the stadium, particularly later in the year. He would have had a big smile on his face."

On defense, the Giants smothered quarterback Mark Brunell, as the league's second-ranked offense went down meekly with a paltry 125 net yards and no points.

"They played possessed," general manager Ernie Accorsi said of the Giants defense, "and no one can convince me their feelings for Mr. Mara didn't have something to do with it."

Afterward, John positioned himself just inside the door of the Giants locker room, the exact spot his father—in victory and defeat—stood so many times, greeting his beloved team after each game. Eli Manning presented John with the game ball in a teary moment.

"Kind of the passing of the torch," center Shaun O'Hara said.

"It was pretty special," John said. "I said, 'Don't do this to me. I don't know if I can hold my emotions any more than I have this week.' Obviously, it's very gratifying."

Three weeks later, the Giants, on their home field, defeated the Eagles 27-17. It was six days after the death of Tisch, who purchased half of the Giants from the Mara family following the 1990 season and ever since had been a calming, unpretentious supporter. Once again, there was a warm locker room ceremony, this time Barber and Manning presenting sons Steven and Jonathan Tisch with the game ball.

"The only way that we truly—and we talked about this—show the Tisch family how much we cared for and loved Bob Tisch was through our actions on the field," Coughlin said. "Words don't get it done."

Twice, the Giants were able to overcome a groundswell of sadness to win a game they desperately wanted and needed.

"As convoluted as it sounds, I think it gives us an emotional lift instead of an emotional downer," Barber said of the deaths of Mara and Tisch. "It gives us inspiration and celebration of what they meant as men to this league and to this game, especially to our team."

THE COACHES

Allie and Vince

Following the 1953 season, Wellington Mara made what he called "the hardest decision I'd ever made" when, along with his brother Jack, he fired Steve Owen after 23 years as the head coach.

"That was like telling your father to move out," Mara said. "He was with us for so long and like a father figure."

Allie Sherman figured he'd be the next head coach. After all, since 1949 Sherman had been one of Owen's three full-time assistants. But Sherman received a call from Jack Mara telling him that Jim Lee Howell, who split time as a Giants assistant and serving as the head coach at Wagner College, was getting the job.

Both Mara and Howell wanted Sherman to stay as an assistant, but Sherman realized he needed a change of scenery to advance his career. He landed his first head-coaching gig not in New York, but in Winnipeg of the Canadian Football League.

The Jewish kid from Brooklyn, along with his wife, Joan, and six-month-old son, Randy, packed up and headed north.

"That given day when we left from the airport, it was a lovely summer day, I was the most hated mortal on this globe," Sherman said. "On one side, for Joanie's parents, this is their first grandchild that I'm taking to another country. On the other side, were my

Allie Sherman (Photo courtesy of the New York Giants)

parents, and I'm taking away their first grandchild. I guess either side would have killed me if they could."

Three years later, Sherman returned to his role as a Giants assistant after making a pact with himself that he would never again remove his family from its roots. In 1961 he replaced Howell as the head coach, but only after the team first tried to lure one of its former assistants, Vince Lombardi, back from Green Bay.

Lombardi left the Giants to coach the Packers in 1959, and before departing he tried to take Sherman with him. "Vince was going to go to Green Bay to talk to them about the job," Sherman said. "He said to me, 'Don't go anywhere, I'm going to go down there, I'm going to take that job and you're gonna come with me.' I said, 'No, Vince.' I had made up my mind. He said, 'What do you mean no? You come down there, I'll get you the same money I have. What do you want? You want defense, I'll take offense, you want offense, I'll take defense. We'll knock the shit out of this league.' I said, 'No, I don't want to leave New York.'

"I would have loved to have done it. We were closer than people realized. People thought we were adversaries, yeah, we were, on the field, shit yes. But off the field, no."

Hats Off to Landry

Before he was a Texas icon, wearing the famous fedora and stoic expression, before he was a Hall of Famer or a Super Bowl-winning coach, Tom Landry spent six years (1954-59) as an assistant coach with the Giants under Jim Lee Howell.

Landry directed some of the finest defensive units the Giants ever assembled.

"Landry was the best," said Dick Lynch, a starting cornerback at the time. "He was the sharpest coach we ever had. We look at the formation, we know the yards, what the down was, how much time was on the clock, what's the score. We could figure out the play. We'd read our keys and if they did a certain thing, this guy was going to do a certain thing. Bang, bang, bang.

"He used to talk very softly, never said a curse word. He used to get it into your head, this is the way it's going to be. He'd say, 'If he goes out in the flat, anticipate him going down and in.' I'd say, 'What if he goes out and he doesn't go down and in?' He'd say, 'Dick, if he goes out, he's going down and in.' I'd say, 'What if he goes down and in and back out?' He said, 'If that happens, then I'll take responsibility.' He used to get you thinking, to always anticipate."

The Deal That Saved a Career

In the annals of Giants history, the name Ed Kolman is not listed with the greats who helped shape the franchise. He was an offensive line assistant coach for 13 seasons, starting in 1950 and, after a brief interruption, ending in 1965. He put in his time, came and left. Yet he made a contribution that changed the direction of the team.

Ed Kolman saved the career of linebacker Sam Huff.

Ed Kolman?

As a rookie in 1956, Huff was making $7,500 and wasn't enjoying his first taste of life in the NFL. His head coach, Jim Lee Howell, screamed at all the rookies and Huff was no exception. Huff was playing on both the offensive and defensive lines and figured all the abuse wasn't worth it.

"I was going to leave, because school teachers were making more money than professional football players, if you can believe it," said Huff.

Huff, who grew up in a West Virginia coal mining camp, wanted to go home. "It just wasn't fun," he said. "It was hard work and Jim Lee Howell yelling at you all the time, screaming at you. Hell, I was not used to that.

"It was a mistake I almost made. When Ed Kolman found out I was going to leave he came to my room and talked with me, he was the first one to ever say to me, 'Sam, this will be the biggest mistake in your life if you leave this camp.' He said, 'You can play in this league and you'll be a big star in this league.' I had a lot of respect for him because he was a great player with the Chicago Bears."

The words inspired Huff but did not completely convince him to stay. He knew at daybreak he'd again incur the wrath of Howell.

"Yelling at me was not the way to motivate me," Huff said. "Never has been, never will be. That is one thing I do not allow, somebody to get in my face and yell at me. Nobody ever wants to do that."

An accord was struck that summer night.

"Ed Kolman told me, 'If you stay, he won't yell at you again. I'll talk to him and he will not yell at you again,'" Huff said. "I said, 'You got a deal.'"

Huff remained with the Giants and a Hall of Fame career was saved.

Two Who Got Away

Talk about your dream team. In the history of professional football, was there ever an assistant coaching tandem as formidable as the duo the Giants employed from 1954 to 1958?

Tom Landry for the defense, Vince Lombardi for the offense, both on the Giants scene long before their Hall of Fame careers took wing.

How in the world did the Giants let Lombardi leave for Green Bay in 1959 and allow Landry to head to Dallas in 1960?

"I always regretted that the situation was such that we couldn't keep either Lombardi or Landry on our staffs," owner Wellington Mara said. "We all recognized they were both great head-coaching material."

Jim Lee Howell was the Giants' head coach at the time and did not have a losing season in his seven years. Mara, ever loyal, wouldn't jettison a winning coach, even for a white-hot prospect.

"Lombardi was always looking for a head-coaching job, he explored a lot of them," Mara said. "In fact, I talked him out of one or two I didn't think would be right for him. When Green Bay was interested in him, I knew that was the place for him to go."

That left Landry.

"Landry was leaving, he was going to get a job coaching the Houston team in the American League, which was just starting up," Mara said. "I offered him the Giants job, because by that time Jim Lee Howell was leaving, it was the first time I ever heard the expression 'burnout.' Jim Lee said the eight victories don't make up for the two defeats.

"I tried to get Landry to take the job and I always remember, he said, 'No, I have a chance to go back home, you know I'm a Texan.' He left, and he wasn't out the door 10 minutes when I picked up the phone and called [Dallas Cowboys president] Tex Schramm and said 'This guy, we're losing him, I don't want him going to the other league, you're still looking for a coach, and I think you ought to hire him.'"

Years later, Mara felt the sting again. "Losing an outstanding guy like John Fox," he said, alluding to the Giants' defensive coordinator under Jim Fassel. Fox was hired by the Carolina Panthers in 2002. "You hated to see him go but you had a coach here who was under contract working hard for you."

Lombardi was in Green Bay for two years when Howell decided to retire following the 1960 season. Mara wanted to bring Lombardi back. "He was wild to come back," Mara said. "But he had only been there two years, and he said, 'I don't feel I fulfilled my promise here, I just don't think I can do that to these people.'

I always suspected that Lombardi also knew he had a damn good team coming along. But he really regretted not coming back. Once later on in his career he tried to come back here, but we had Allie Sherman, who was doing a very good job, and we had our loyalties.

"I always regretted losing those two. The timing just didn't work out."

No Fan of Mail

As the public relations director of the Giants, it was Don Smith's job to promote the team. Or so he thought.

Smith traveled to Los Angeles on a Tuesday to advance that Sunday's 1959 season opener against the Rams and came up with what he thought was an unusual way to show just how big a celebrity Sam Huff was, nationally as well as in New York. Huff at middle linebacker was the glamour boy of the rugged Giants defense in the late '50s and early '60s.

Purchasing a penny postcard, Smith wrote "#70" on the card. That's it. No name, no address, no city, no state. Nothing. Just Huff's uniform number. Then he dropped the card in a mailbox on Wilshire Boulevard. A week later, the card wound up clear across the country, landing in a pile of fan mail at Huff's locker inside Yankee Stadium.

"Went through the entire postal system, nothing on it but number 70," Smith said proudly.

The postcard deal got Smith thinking. He phoned Jack Hand, a veteran wire-service writer at the Associated Press, and recounted the story. Hand loved it but didn't believe it. "So I showed him the card with the postmarks," Smith said. "He wrote a story about it."

Smith was feeling mighty triumphant until head coach Allie Sherman took notice.

"Allie was an offensive guy, he loved the offense, he tolerated the defense and he hated those guys because he thought they were [defensive coordinator] Tom Landry's. The Landry ghost was always there with him.

"Allie calls me in his office, he says, 'What the hell right do you have to put a story out about Sam Huff?' I said, 'Allie, the Giants pay me to get publicity for the team. This is a story that got on the national AP wire all across the country.' He said, 'I don't want this guy Huff being made some kind of a demigod, he's no better than any other player on the team.' He never forgave me for that. He thought I was taking the defense and elevating it and making a hero out of one of them, but the guy was a hero without me making him one."

Goodbye, Allie

Do not think for a moment that after eight years as head coach, time finally running out on Allie Sherman had nothing to do with the rise of the Jets as the hot team in New York.

In his final year, the Giants were sitting pretty at 7-3 in 1968 before a mighty thud.

"We were within range of a playoff spot, we wound up losing our last four games of the season," Sherman said. "Meanwhile, of course, the Jets caught fire."

The Jets, the AFL team sharing the same city as the Giants, sure did take off. They never stopped soaring until they beat the Colts in Super Bowl III, one of the greatest upsets in sports history.

"Joe [Namath] guaranteed they would win, and they did," Sherman said, "and it was the game that not only guaranteed his legend forever, it officially gave us a status we'd never had before: We were the No. 2 team in New York. We were The Other Guys. And it only got worse."

The following summer, the Giants were on their way to an 0-5 preseason when on August 17 they faced the Jets at the Yale Bowl in New Haven, Connecticut. It was the first ever game between these two teams and no one would dare say it didn't mean anything. This was the same weekend as the Woodstock Musical Festival in upstate Bethel, New York, and while the youth of the nation was turning on, Sherman's Giants were bottoming out.

"I was under enormous pressure by then," Sherman said. "Wellington Mara, who had been reassuring through all the difficult times in 1964 and 1966, was under just as much stress. The Jets were hot. We were hurting. They had Namath. We didn't. They beat us, 37-14. Three weeks later, Well called me with the news."

During the previous season, the restless Giants fans began chanting for Sherman's firing, singing "Goodbye Allie" to the tune of "Goodnight Ladies." It got ugly and also more creative.

"They had a house band at Yankee Stadium that played 'Bye Bye Blackbird' every week," said Ed Croke, at the time a public relations assistant. "When it got to the chorus, the whole fucking stadium sang, 'Bye Bye, Allie.'"

On September 11, the Giants lost to the Steelers 17-13 in the preseason finale in Montreal, and Giants fans up north mockingly sang "Au revoir, Allie" as a final and French serenade to Sherman.

"Sherman was getting threats to his life and his kids were getting beat up in school," said Don Smith, the public relations director. "He was a basket case at the end. It was bad. The next morning Wellington Mara called me and said, 'Get in early, were naming a new coach today.'"

Tough Big Red

At an offseason banquet, Don Smith—the Giants' public relations director—happened to be sitting next to Gino Marchetti, the famed Colts defensive end who was not only a Hall of Famer but was also renowned as one of the NFL's all-time tough guys.

"Guys used to die when he came after them," Smith said.

The two struck up a conversation, and Smith wanted to know: Was Marchetti upset about his reputation as a menacing individual?

"He said, 'Well, not really, because I'm not the toughest guy in this league,'" Smith recalled. "He told me the toughest guy in this league was Alex Webster, that he wouldn't go near him in a fight. This was incredible to me, because Alex was this big teddy bear who we all loved. Marchetti said Webster was the toughest son of a bitch who ever walked the face of the earth."

Smith could not believe it. Alex Webster? The unassuming former Giants fullback who in 1969 took over as head coach for Allie Sherman? Alex Webster, who was affectionately known as "Big Red?"

"He was a big, burly guy and the most docile, nice, warm, and fuzzy guy you can ever meet," Smith said. "He just was a pleasure."

How could this lovable guy be such a brute?

Smith couldn't figure it out.

For a short while, the move to Webster looked to be inspired as the Giants won three of their first four games. Then they lost seven straight.

"Alex was an easygoing guy, he tolerated a lot of stuff in practice, guys would do things and he didn't care, they'd miss meetings," Smith said. "He wasn't a disciplinarian, and he was still a ballplayer at heart. They took advantage of him and stopped playing well. Alex took a look at this, and he thought it was a direct insult to the way he had treated them. He had lost control of the team in a sense."

Through it all, Smith remained curious and kept Marchetti's words about Webster filed away in his mind. One day, after a light workout at Yankee Stadium during the losing streak, Webster cleared the media out of the locker room for a private team meeting. Smith at the time was in a small alcove tucked in the back of the room. Webster slammed the locker room door shut with Smith still inside.

"I'm in the back of this damn room, I can't get out," Smith said. "I'm hiding."

Webster told everyone to sit down.

According to Smith, Webster said, "You guys are taking advantage of me, you think I'm a pushover. I tell you what, if I'm gonna be the leader of this team I have to be the toughest guy, so I'm gonna take you guys on right now, one at a time or the whole goddamn bunch of you. Nothing will ever be said about it. We'll see who the best man is. I'll kick the shit out of all of you."

Smith was as stunned as the players.

"These guys were sitting in their cubicles and they weren't even breathing," Smith said. "He was like a madman. Alex went out into the hall and closed the door and waited out there. I'm inside and I'm watching all these guys around the corner, and they're not moving. The door opened and Alex would say, 'All right, three of you, c'mon out,' he'd go down the line, 'How about you? You think you're so tough? I'll take you and break you in half.' This went on for a half hour and those guys never moved. Finally he said, 'We got that decided, who's the toughest guy.' "

No punches were ever thrown, but Smith that day got a clear picture of why Gino Marchetti thought Alex Webster was so tough.

The Beer Necessities

Avoid the head coach. That's the objective for night-owl players slipping back into the team hotel (shame, shame) just after curfew the night before a road game.

Or, when Alex Webster was the coach, the goal was avoid him if you wanted to get to bed BEFORE curfew.

Alex Webster (Photo courtesy of the New York Giants)

"We went to play San Francisco [in 1972], and Ron Johnson and I are coming back to the hotel," tight end Bob Tucker said.

"We were roommates, we were walking in at about 10:30 p.m., our curfew was at 11, and Joe Walton, our offensive coach and Alex were at the bar," Johnson said.

Tucker: "Alex says, 'C'mon guys, let's have a drink.' "

Johnson: "Mr. Webster was a rabble-rouser as a player and stayed the same way as a coach."

Tucker: "We said, 'No, we're going upstairs,' he says, 'Nah, goddamn, you're coming into the bar with me.' So we go into the bar, Alex is having a few cocktails, Ron and I are not drinking, we're having a Coke or something, we're sitting there talking, next thing you know it's 11 o'clock, then 11:15.

"We say, 'Alex, we got to go to bed.' He says, 'You're not going anywhere. Bring a round over here.' Wouldn't let us go."

The night turned to morning.

Johnson: "I think we got out of there at one o'clock. He knew us, he respected us. We did fine. What's a couple of hours?"

There was a game to play.

Tucker: "We went out that afternoon and kicked their ass."

Final score: Giants 23, 49ers 17.

The Heat Is (Off)

The son of the owner is not supposed to be thrust into awkward situations by employees, but John Mara found himself smack dab in the middle of an uncomfortable moment during the final game of the miserable 1973 season.

"We're having a terrible year, playing at the Yale Bowl and Alex Webster had announced prior to the last game of the season that he was going to retire," Mara said. "I think he knew pretty much we were going to have to make a change. We were playing Minnesota, and at halftime of that game, we're getting beat pretty badly and I can remember him coming up to me in the trainer's room and he was in tears, saying to me, 'I'm sorry I couldn't bring your family a winner, I did the best I could.'

"He hugged me at the time, and I remember feeling like I wanted to cry myself, it was as emotional as I'd ever seen him."

Webster's last game did not go well, as the Giants were on their way to a 31-7 loss to the Vikings to close out a 2-11-1 season.

"The second half of the game, it was a completely one-sided affair, and it was very cold," Mara said. "Most of the players seemed to be huddled around the bench, around a couple of these portable heaters that we had to keep 'em warm, and they weren't really paying attention to what was going on, they weren't really into the game at all. So at one point Alex called me over, I was on the bench in those days, and he said, 'Go over and disconnect those heaters, I want these guys paying attention, I want to go down with a fight and not huddled around a bench.'

"So I went over and pulled the plug on these two portable heaters and the players are looking at me, some of 'em screaming obscenities at me. There was Ron Johnson and Carl Lockhart, who I was friendly with, they were extremely upset with me. Looking back on it, I can't blame them."

Wrong Man for the Job

The last one to know he's not right for the job is usually the person in that job. Not so with Alex Webster, and not so for his wife.

Webster ran the show as the head coach of the Giants from 1969 through the 1973 season. He was a well-liked, fun-loving former Giants player and a popular choice. But it did not turn out to be a wise or inspired choice.

"I think what happened was he was not ready for it, and he will admit that himself," said Louise Webster, married to Alex for more than 50 years. "He sort of got pushed into it. He's not the type to be a coach. He just doesn't know how to be tough, and you have to be as a coach, and the players just walked all over him. He treated the players like he wanted to be treated and that wasn't what the players needed at that time."

That fairly accurately sums up Webster's four years at the helm. His career record was 29-40-1, but he wasn't a total failure.

In 1970, the Giants went 9-5 and were in playoff contention until the final week of the season. Webster, following that campaign, was even named NFL Coach of the Year by the Washington D.C. Touchdown Club.

Yet Webster knew he wasn't a perfect fit as the head coach.

"To me when you come to work, especially in football, you don't clown around," Webster said. "Guys pull jokes and stunts and all that, but you got to be serious. I guess I just didn't have enough experience to take it. It got to me after a while. I loved the kids. That was my problem.

"I had a couple of good years. We were on the right track; we just didn't have any depth. The league had changed, everybody got the big backs and big linemen and we just got overpowered by a lot of teams. We just couldn't keep up with 'em. We could score points, but defensively we had a tough time stopping everybody."

An Unwelcome Change

As far as personality traits, the move from Alex Webster as head coach of the Giants to Bill Arnsparger could not have been more glaring. Where Webster was gregarious, Arnsparger was reclusive. Where Webster was loose, Arnsparger was tight.

In the NFL standings, the switch from Webster in 1973 (2-11-1) to Arnsparger in 1974 (2-12) was negligible. But to those who had to deal with one and then the other, the difference was startling.

"That was a huge change," running back Ron Johnson said. "You went from somebody who was very user-friendly to somebody who, I don't know how to put this, I don't think had the same understanding of people skills that Alex had.

"For whatever reason we really got off to a very, very bad start with each other. He was dealing with a very cocky young black man in me, and I didn't want to be looked down upon. He wanted to enforce his rules. Alex knew all of his players and knew what limits he could take, but with Bill Arnsparger it was one rule and everybody had to follow those rules."

Johnson, the team's leading rusher the previous two years, learned quickly about life under Arnsparger.

"[Tight end] Bob Tucker and I used to play chess all the time," Johnson said. "Literally, sometimes the guys would be running out on the field to get ready to start the game and we were still moving chess pieces. Everybody used to tease us, that's all we did all the time. It was in a training camp and Bob and I came into a meeting five minutes late.

"You know what, should we have been fined? Yes, we should have been fined. Would Alex have fined us? No, he probably would have made an example out of us and made a joke about it. Arnsparger fined me and did not fine Bob Tucker. Obviously I was not too quiet about it, raised a lot of heck about it."

A Grand Worth Losing

This is Bob Tuckers take on what Bill Arnsparger contributed to the Giants during his relatively brief tenure as head coach: "Arnsparger destroyed the tradition of the New York Giants," Tucker stated, "and that's not an easy thing to do."

Not exactly a glowing endorsement.

One of the changes that Tucker absolutely abhorred was Arnsparger's decision to take the play-calling away from the quarterback and the use of a shuttle system to get the plays into the huddle.

The time came when Tucker was asked to shuttle plays onto the field. During a game against the Cowboys, the Giants trailed in Dallas by 10 points when Arnsparger gave the play to Tucker.

From left: Andy Robustelli, Bill Arnsparger, and Wellington Mara (Photo courtesy of the New York Giants)

"Third down and 12 he gives me this stupid running play," Tucker said. "I figure the hell with that, so I made up my own play. I gave it to the quarterback, it was a pass play, and I said, 'Bill said to look for me deep.' The quarterback kind of stared at me because he knew Bill wouldn't say such a thing. I said, 'Yeah, I can't believe it myself.' I knew what defense we were gonna get, it was a double zone and the middle was gonna be wide open and he threw the ball and we score, I went like 50 yards for a touchdown. We kick the extra point, I come back to the sideline and Arnsparger was in my face, yelling and screaming at me and fined me $1,000 for changing the play.

"It was the best $1,000 I ever spent, because he didn't ask me to run in another play ever."

The Brush-Off

Be careful what you wish for.

In 1974, the Giants could not believe their great fortune when they landed Bill Arnsparger, the architect of the renowned Dolphins' 53 Defense, as their new head coach. "We thought this was the hire of the century," said John Mara, son of owner Wellington Mara.

It turned out to be one of the worst misjudgments in franchise history. Arnsparger was a gifted assistant but an abysmal head coach.

"I remember my first impression of Bill Arnsparger," Mara said. "It's very early in the training camp in 1974, I was working as an intern in the public relations department. It was my job to help the reporters get a player they wanted for an interview. There was some rookie that this reporter wanted to talk to, and I hadn't learned all the names and faces as of yet, so I went up to Arnsparger and I said, 'Coach, can you tell me who so-and-so is,' and he looked at me and said, 'Learn the personnel, John, learn the personnel.'

"And then he just kept eating. I thought one of two things, either this guy is a complete nut job or he doesn't know who this player is either. I'm not sure which one is accurate, to this day. I was a nobody, but I still was the owner's son. I thought he would have at least made some attempt to answer my question, but he barely even looked at me."

When he was fired seven games into the 1976 season, Arnsparger's record with the Giants was 7-28. His winning percentage of .200 stands as the lowest of any coach in team history.

Do as I Say, Not as He Did

Coaches are often shameless when it comes to finding new and creative ways to motivate their teams. Sometimes they strike gold, other times they strike out. Back in 1980, Ray Perkins took a swing, and missed, badly.

Mired in a five-game losing streak, Perkins was not adverse to using anything in his power to shake the Giants out of their doldrums. The team flew out to San Diego on a Friday for a game two days later against the Chargers, and Perkins figured a little pep talk was in order. He told the Giants of a boxer he once saw named Yaqui Lopez, an overachiever who got the hell beat out of him for 14 rounds, a fighter who had no business still standing.

"Ray said, 'The guy was bleeding, people were yelling 'Stop the fight!' but the guy kept persevering,'" punter Dave Jennings said. "And the guy came out in the 15th round and knocked out his opponent."

Perkins hoped his club could show the same resiliency Lopez showed in that bout. "He said, 'That's the kind of guy I want my players to be, they'll get beat up but they'll come back and win,'" Jennings said.

The tale was not only rousing, but also timely. Lopez was scheduled to fight against Michael Spinks, on national television, on that very Saturday. The tale piqued some interest and many of the players, following a brief walk-through practice, headed back to their hotel rooms in San Diego to see this tough Lopez in action, see the kind of competitor Perkins wanted the Giants to emulate.

"So everybody's kind of interested in this, we went back to the hotel, sat down, had the popcorn, soda," Jennings said. "The guy got blown out."

Spinks battered Lopez, winning on a seventh-round TKO.

"That was an omen of things to come," Jennings said, "because we lost the next day 44-7. It was like hand in hand. It was a perfect set-up, he wants tough guys, guys who won't quit. The guy got knocked out."

"He Was Trying to Kill Us"

Even though it was only preseason, this was going to be a difficult game. On August 11, 1979, the Giants played at Pittsburgh, and not only were the Steelers the defending NFL champions, this was their first home game at Three Rivers Stadium since defeating the Cowboys in Super Bowl VIII.

Naturally, the joint was jumping.

"So when we came in there and they introduced the Steelers, it gave me a chill, the fans gave the Steelers a 15-minute standing ovation," said running back Billy Taylor, who at the time was entering his second year in the league. "I'd never seen anything like that. Jack Lambert and Joe Greene and all those guys."

The Steelers were a great team, the Giants most assuredly were not. Struggling in that difficult environment, the Giants lost 10-3. Their head coach, Ray Perkins, could not accept the defeat.

"The very next morning, we practiced," Taylor said. "We were supposed to have a day off. And he just killed us again. It made me think he doesn't give a shit about me. That's when I got turned off against Perkins. I think I left some of my best games on the practice field. I've never been mad at anybody for making me work hard, but I just thought he was trying to kill us."

No One's Indispensable

There's nothing like the formal presentation of a championship ring to make a player feel on top of the world. Unless, of course, it is Bill Parcells handing out those coveted pieces of jewelry. Then, the experience is considerably more humbling.

"After we won our 1986 Super Bowl we're going into mini-camp in May of 1987, the veterans along with the rookies," cornerback Mark Collins said. "We never had a big ring ceremony, so after we did our mini-camp at Giants Stadium we all walked in as a team into our meeting room, in our sweats, all sweaty and stinky, and we have our ceremony inside the room.

"Parcells calls all the players to get their rings. OK, here's Phil Simms, and we're happy, clapping, yeah, we got our championship rings. And after he finished passing out the rings Parcells cleared his throat on his podium."

Collins figured the head coach would laud the returning players for their great success the prior season.

Parcells didn't do any lauding.

Here's the way Collins recounts the Parcells message that day:

" 'Now listen, all you rookies in here, I don't need any of you son of a bitches on my team.' He said, 'Do I, Phil Simms?' and Phil said, 'Nope.' "

Collins was stunned.

"I'm going into my second year," he said, "and I'm going to myself, 'Wow, what a statement.' How can you demoralize a guy like that? A coach tells you, 'I don't need you, I got my team.' "

Collins knew how unsettled the ring ceremony made him feel. He sought out teammates to learn their reaction.

"I asked Mark Ingram, who was a rookie at the time, 'Man, how did you feel when he said that to you?' " Collins said. "Ingram said, 'He made me feel like I was nothing, he made me feel like

I didn't even exist, and I'm a first-round pick. It motivated me to make me want to prove him wrong, to show that he needed me, that I do count.'"

Message delivered, message received.

Who, Me?

By 1986, George Martin figured he knew all there was to know about Bill Parcells, but the defensive end, entering his 12th NFL season, learned the hard way that his education was far from complete.

"I was feeling pretty cocky and pretty self-assured about myself," Martin said. "We had just drafted Eric Dorsey out of Notre Dame, Eric was a number-one draft choice, getting a lot of money. Obviously he was the envy of all of the team. He also was subject to a lot of ridicule, because he was this unproven rookie coming in getting all this money.

"We delighted in his misery, needless to say. So one day in practice Eric is having a problem grasping all of the terminology and so forth, and he's concentrating so hard on it that he jumps off-sides. That's a cardinal sin, if you know Bill Parcells. As veterans, we're perched over on the sidelines and we're really getting a kick out of this, Eric Dorsey jumping off-sides and getting his comeuppance. After all, who does this brash young upstart think he is?

"So, midway through practice he jumps off-sides again. Parcells, you can see he's like a volcano, he's slowly about to erupt. The veterans, and I was a senior veteran at the time, we're just waiting for the top to blow off.

"Wouldn't you know it, before practice is over Dorsey jumps off the third time. Parcells calls everybody up in a huddle formation and we all know, this is it. Dorsey is gonna get crucified. Parcells begins to rant and rave and he calls me out to the center of the huddle. I think he's calling me out to say, you know, it's unfair to a veteran like George, follow his example.

"Parcells says, 'This is a disgrace, it's a shame the way our team's performing, this is unacceptable and we won't have it. And George Martin, I hold you personally responsible!' He proceeded to, I mean up one side of me and down the other, tear me a brand-new you-know-what."

A stunned Martin could not fathom why he was getting ripped for the failings of some rookie.

"But his point was absolutely brilliant," Martin observed. "After practice was done and everybody was gone he comes over and puts his arm around me and says, 'George, if they think there are no sacred cows everybody will be in line. Besides, you are the veteran on this team, you are the one who will reap the most benefit, you shouldn't accept one of your colleagues, one of your teammates, one of your fellow defensive linemen, one of these rookies giving less than their best, and I expect that kind of leadership from you.' He happened to be right, other than the fact I was fuming at the time."

Indeed, there was a method to Parcells' seeming madness.

"I will tell you this, if it wasn't for George Martin, I don't think Bill Parcells would have had a chance to be successful with the Giants," Parcells said. "He let me, without complaint, with support, do a lot of things I tried to do, particularly early, to get things established the way we needed to."

The Other Bill

In time, Bill Parcells evolved into the superior coach and out-sized personality that made him a very public presence. Few, however, got to know Parcells the way Ed Croke did.

"To this day I can spend two, three days with him and never once talk about his football team," said Croke, the Giants director of public relations throughout Parcells' entire tenure with the team. "He's got too much to say, he's an interesting guy, the guy could have been a CEO of a Fortune 500 company, he's that smart."

The two would more likely be engaged in conversation about Little Anthony and the Imperials or baseball trivia than anything having to do with players or punts or personnel.

"In all honesty, during the season, as tough as it was, we had a little routine we used to do all the time," Croke said. "I like getting in early, he used to get in there 4:30, five o'clock, I'd either go to his office or he'd come to mine, we'd have our coffee and we'd just start bullshitting about who was playing baseball the day before, what did I think about this pitcher, and he'd go, 'I got you, give me the starting infield of the '56 Cleveland Indians.' We'd do lyrics from any kind of '50s music, he'd say, 'Let's see if you know the lyrics from Fats Waller's 'Ain't Misbehavin'.'"

"The last thing we'd do, he'd say, 'By the way, who's coming by today?' and I'd say 'Well, this guy wants to talk to you but ignore him, he's a pain in the ass, but you got to do this or this guy needs you to give him 15 minutes.'"

Getting His Phil

The play would end and the battle would commence. Bill Parcells vs. Phil Simms. So often, before he even made it to the sideline, Simms could sense, feel, and hear Parcells barking at him.

"Jeff Rutledge and Jeff Hostetler would be standing behind him and Bill would just go, 'And Simms,' and I haven't even said nothing," Simms said, "but I guess he could see it in my face and my hand gestures that I'm getting ready to say something. He goes,

'You just shut up, you play and I'll coach,' and of course it would be colorful. As he would say it, the two quarterbacks would stay behind him and they would just smile and laugh and point at me, it just made their day to hear him kill me like that.

"I'd just go, 'OK, what do you want to tell me?' He'd go, 'Here's what I want to tell you, you go out there and tell those SOBs I said they better block for you. And here's what I want, don't take a sack and damn it don't throw an interception and whatever you do, don't fumble the damn ball.' I'm like, 'OK, I didn't know these things, thanks for reminding me.'"

The relationship was turbulent but grounded in mutual respect. That doesn't mean it was always pleasant.

"It was always 'F-ing Simms this, f-ing Simms that,'" Simms said. "Unfortunately, we do have a lot of similarities, and if I were a coach I would coach somewhat in his style. I don't think I could do the fear thing as good as him.

"Yes, we did argue, and people ask me were we close? I don't think we were all that close. I was a player and he was my coach. I never felt comfortable in the eight years I was with him. It was hard."

No Idle Chatter

Mark Collins was full of himself when he arrived in 1986 as the Giants' second-round draft pick out of Fullerton State. The best cornerbacks carry themselves with an air of invulnerability and show no fear, and Collins, even as an untested rookie, fit that description.

"I walked in cocky and conceited; I was very self-assured and self-confident that I could get the job done," Collins said.

Naturally, Bill Parcells didn't take kindly to the bravado Collins displayed on a daily basis.

Mark Collins (Mike Powell/Getty Images)

"Don't forget, they had Mark Haynes there and they traded him to the Denver Broncos, and I was the next guy in line," Collins said. "I don't think Bill really liked that too much."

Collins earned a starting job in his very first year on an outstanding defensive unit that spearheaded the push to a 14-2 regular season and ultimate victory in Super Bowl XXI. Along the way, Collins never shed his cloak of confidence and never quite warmed up to Parcells' heavy-handed coaching methods.

"Me and Bill never had a great relationship," Collins said. "He said it even in his book, a question was asked of him, who was the toughest player you've ever been on and he said Mark Collins. He said, 'Because I never really let him know how good a player he really was.' We never talked about anything. I didn't want Bill to like me, and conversely, I really didn't like him that much. The one thing that bonded us was our mutual respect. It wasn't a hate relationship, we just didn't talk. But we got the job done and later, I guess as we evolved we developed even more mutual respect for each other, about my game and his coaching abilities.

"I always quote Parcells because he is THE best coach I ever worked for. Do I like him? I like what he's done, because I really don't know him still."

Ties That Bind

During his eight years as head coach of the Giants, Bill Parcells won two Super Bowls and established himself as a premier coach. He hopes his legacy is a simple one.

"I just would hope most of the players believed I was trying to win every game I played, preseason, regular season, I never put a percentage on the competition of the moment," Parcells said. "I tried to maintain a team's constant dedication toward playing to their potential. I'm still trying to do it. At least this guy was trying to give his players a chance to win. That's what I would hope they would think I was about."

When Parcells thinks back on his two championship teams, he sees relationships and shared experiences that will not fade as the years go by.

"We kind of had our own band of guys in those days," Parcells said. "What I've been happy to see is the relationships of those players have been maintained for long periods of time. That's when you know you really had a team, because those guys still like each other, they still see each other, they still help each other.

"That's one thing about that era of the Giants when I was there, the best way to put it is this, when you've won there's something that bonds you together and it's just inexplicable to people who haven't been there. It creates a blood kinship. The best thing about it is that there are no rules and regulations about it, it's even better than a family because there's no criteria on it. It's just that feeling you have about that group of guys. There's no standard, if you're in, you're in, if you're not in, you're not in. You're just bonded together by that, bonded together for life."

Should Have Known

There is no other way to characterize Ray Handley's two-year stay as head coach as anything but a complete embarrassment. The Giants have suffered through worse seasons (8-8 in 1991, 6-10 in 1992) but it was the way they lost, the way Handley lost control of the team, the way players openly mutinied that made this an era of error, a reign of ruin.

Before Handley ever coached a single game, there were indications that he was going to flop.

"I get called into his office, he wants to meet me after he gets named head coach," said Bob Papa, then the Giants' pregame and postgame radio host on WNEW-AM. "He looks up from his desk, those glasses, he always had his face buried in some notes or some stats. 'Coach, thanks for having me in, what did you want to talk about?' He goes, 'I know what you do.'

"It was very Nixon-esque. He says, 'You do that pregame show and that postgame show, we all listen to that postgame show on the way home from games. I want you to go easy on us.' He was trying to set parameters for the show. I'm like, 'Coach, you got a defending Super Bowl team.' He was so paranoid and so freaked out already about what was going to be on the Giants' postgame show in five months. It was like Captain Queeg. I walked out of his office and I'm like, 'We're in for a long haul.'"

Ray Handley (Photo courtesy of the New York Giants)

No Ray of Hope

As the director of public relations, Ed Croke was supposed to help present a positive image for Ray Handley when he took over for Bill Parcells in 1991. Soon enough, Croke learned this was mission impossible.

"He wasn't a lot of fun to work with, at all," Croke said. "Not a joy. He was more interested in reading the *Wall Street Journal* than he was in coaching, anyway. He was a genius in the stock market. He was a professional card counter, he got banned from the gambling casinos in Las Vegas. Somebody that preoccupied with counting cards and the stock market isn't spending a lot of time learning about Xs and Os."

Croke tried to navigate Handley, who lasted only two seasons, through the murky waters, but never came close to getting the beleaguered coach to shore. On one particularly gristly afternoon, Handley ran afoul of his senses and the truth when he shoved Joe Gigli, a photographer from the Newark *Star-Ledger,* in a fit of anger.

Handley did not allow the photographers inside the fence during practice, but Gigli and Keith Torrie, a photographer from the *New York Daily News,* clicked a few shots of Handley through an opening in the gate. Incensed, Handley castigated the two and brushed past Gigli, pushing him out of the way. Torrie, an innocent bystander, did his job and got a picture of Handley putting his hands on Gigli.

"Handley kept saying, 'I never touched him,'" Torrie said, "and there he is in a picture touching him on the back page."

This was not a good situation.

"I went down to his office to confront Ray," Croke said. "I said, 'This is not doing us any good, we're trying to make your image a little bit better.' He fucking went nuts, saying, 'I didn't touch anybody!' I say, 'I wasn't there, I'm just telling you what they tell me. There were enough witnesses there, why are you fucking denying this for?' He went nuts again. That's his story—he said, she said, fine, see you later. The moron tells me he didn't push a photographer when 28 guys saw him do it."

Reeves Peeved

When Dan Reeves was hired by the Giants in 1993, no one ever characterized the marriage as a match made in heaven. General manager George Young settled on Reeves after first offering the job to Tom Coughlin and then Dave Wannstedt. Young knew Reeves was a quality head coach but feared a stormy, long-range forecast. Young's instincts proved to be correct.

In his four years in New York, Reeves experienced more bad than good and never embraced the way the Giants went about their football business. While in Denver, Reeves guided the Broncos to three Super Bowls (all losses) and he did it by picking his own players; he had final say when it came to the NFL Draft. Reeves knew he could not have that power with the Giants, and he often disagreed with Young and Tom Boisture, the team's vice president of player personnel. At times, Reeves chafed when he did not get his way.

"We had some run-ins, that was one of the problems I had, in the personnel part of it," Reeves said. "The biggest one, of course, was the Tyrone Wheatley thing."

The Tyrone Wheatley thing proved to be an embarrassing scenario for all concerned. It was no secret the Giants were looking for a running back in the first round of the 1995 NFL Draft. They took Wheatley, out of Michigan, and almost immediately afterward, word spread of a contentious Giants war room battle. Reeves described the scene as "the most argumentative" he'd ever witnessed.

Reeves preferred another running back, Rashaan Salaam out of Colorado, ahead of Wheatley. The problem was exacerbated when Reeves' opinion became public knowledge. Reeves and Wheatley never gained each other's trust.

"That was just a hard way to start, when all of a sudden it came out that I was against Wheatley and they wanted Wheatley, and I wanted whatever running back, I can't even remember," Reeves said. "That was a bad way to start, I had to try to get Tyrone to understand what wasn't the case, it wasn't like I didn't like him. That should have never come out. That makes it tough on you to coach. Regardless of who makes the decision, everybody needs to be on the same page."

A Fond Adieu

The end of every season is not complete until a player meets with the head coach for an exit interview. These usually are not long, drawn-out discussions but they certainly can create angst in an athlete.

Dan Reeves, anxious to put a wrap on the season, often staged these meetings quite early in the morning; his sessions rarely included any angst.

"He was very up front with you, let you know where you stood, for better or for worse," kicker Brad Daluiso said. "When I first met him and I wasn't kicking field goals he would say early on, 'We'd love for you to develop the field goal thing, that's got to get better.' He certainly didn't just come give you high-fives in those meetings."

Once he established himself as a bonafide NFL kicker, Daluiso's exit interviews with Reeves were memorable for their congeniality.

"When you did have in the NFL what would be considered a tiny bit of stability, if you had a good year, if you're a placekicker, it's a little different than the other positions," Daluiso said. "It's very numbers-oriented, when I was kicking off well and had a good field goal percentage, I'd come in, sit down, the door would shut, and you're kind of waiting for the hammer to drop about something.

"He'd say, 'When are you going back to San Diego?' I'd say, 'I have a flight this afternoon,' and he'd kind of gaze up and, you know how he loves to golf and he loves the warm weather, you could tell he was just kind of fantasizing about me getting back to San Diego. He's say, 'Man, it's nice back there.' I'd say, 'Yeah, it really is, Coach.' He'd say, 'Alright, see you later,' and that would be the meeting. It's a nice way to be sent off."

Jim Dandy

Glenn Parker had been in the league for 10 years before signing with the Giants for the 2000 season, and the shaved-headed offensive guard knew his way around head coaches. But upon arrival in New York he did not know exactly what to expect out of Jim Fassel, other than hearing that Fassel was a pretty good guy.

And then, early in his first training camp with the Giants, Parker learned much more about his new coach. Fassel always hated the label he wore as a "player's coach," because he thought it meant he was too soft, but there was no denying he was well-liked by those who played for him.

"In the preseason in the first year, Fassel in a special teams meeting said, 'Hey guys, what can we do to get better?' and one of our linebackers, Pete Monty, piped up and said, 'Well, it could help if we didn't have such a pussy-ass coach who would allow us to once in a while call a fake.' Right to Fassel. And Fassel just broke out laughing. I was kind of like, 'Oh, hey, I wonder if we've crossed the line here,' and the minute he broke out laughing I was like, 'Oh, that's the type of guy he is.' "

Once he got to know him better, Parker knew he too could kid the coach. "Going into our last year I made fun of him about his neck injury," Parker said. "He went in for neck surgery and I said, 'Coach you can tell people you had some sort of injury to your neck but we really all know it's hurt because you keep snapping back looking over your shoulder to see who's gonna take your job.' There were always those rumors with him. He gave it right back to me."

Hide and Seek

Their offices sat side by side inside Giants Stadium, one belonging to general manager Ernie Accorsi, the other occupied by John Fox, the defensive coordinator. Proximity was only one reason why the two spoke so often. The chatty Fox would sidle up to a dead tree to explain the complexities and nuances of his defensive schemes, while Accorsi, a master storyteller, never met an anecdote he did not relish repeating. The two were made for each other.

Each week during the 2000 season, Fox and Accorsi engaged in casual and at times animated discussion, Fox in great detail and honesty began laying out his gameplan for the upcoming game.

Accorsi looked forward to these informal sessions, but once, he admitted he avoided Fox leading up to one of their most important games. During the second week of January following the 2000 regular season, the Giants were preparing to meet the Vikings in the NFC Championship Game, and Accorsi went out of his way to steer clear of Fox.

"I wouldn't even talk to him, I didn't even want to see him," Accorsi said.

Consider it a willful attempt to hear-no-evil.

Accorsi knew Fox was confronting a great challenge, figuring out a way to contain an array of offensive talent featuring Randy Moss, Cris Carter, Robert Smith, and Daunte Culpepper. The Vikings had scored 397 points that season and showed no signs of slowing down one week earlier in their 34-16 playoff victory over the Saints.

Accorsi was fearful he'd grow too depressed by what Fox had to say.

"He did that all week," Fox said of Accorsi's dodging tactics. "Sometimes when you get on a roll like that, we're all kind of sick, we have superstitions."

Finally, on Friday, the two spoke when Accorsi ventured downstairs to sense the mood of the team during a lunch break. Accorsi didn't dig into the barbeque spread, but he did seek out Fox.

"He had this sheepish look on his face," Fox recalled, "and he said, 'So?' I said, 'We're gonna be just fine.' I really believed it. We just matched up well."

Said Accorsi, "He said, 'I want to tell you something, were going to be fine.' He didn't say were going to shut them out. That really made me feel good, because I had tremendous confidence in him."

The Vikings never had a chance. Fox's defense held the Vikings to nine first downs and 114 total yards in a 41-0 title rout.

All Revved Up

The handwriting was all but spray-painted on the wall. Jim Fassel was going to be fired following the 2003 season and so, on December 17, with two games remaining, Fassel made a request of John Mara, the Giants executive vice president:

Get my job status out in the open.

That was that. A day later, it became public knowledge that the team was set to make a coaching change. While describing the way Fassel forced the issue as "classy," general manager Ernie Accorsi said, "We'll start immediately" when asked about seeking Fassel's replacement. Less than a month later, on January 7, 2004, Tom Coughlin was introduced as the new head coach.

Coughlin arrived with a fire-and-brimstone message, and the Giants, after seven years under Fassel's nurturing guidance, were forewarned: There's a new sheriff in town and he's taking no guff.

Just what could the Giants expect of their new taskmaster? Just listen to Phil McConkey, a Giants receiver when Coughlin was his assistant coach from 1988-90:

"He used to commute with Fred Hoaglin, the offensive line coach, two completely different personalities," McConkey said. "Fred was laid back, smoked cigars, soft-spoken, never raised his voice. Tom is Type A, running around, scurrying here and there. They're on Route 80 one day coming into Giants Stadium, Tom's driving this week, there was a bad accident, the whole highway's shut down, people turn their cars off, got out of the car.

*Tom Coughlin (Photo courtsey of Charles Wenzelberg/*NY Post*)*

"Hoaglin walks out of the car, walks over to the guard rail, takes out a cigar, just leans back, talks to people, makes friends. This thing's going on for an hour. He can see a mile or so ahead the traffic is starting to move, so people are going back to their cars, starting their cars up. He gets back to the car and there's Tom, engine revving, both hands on the steering wheel, looking straight ahead. He'd been in that position for the whole hour. That's him. He was gonna be ready."

Hearing this, Coughlin commended McConkey's memory but offered one slight correction. "You forgot to mention," Coughlin said, "that I never took the car out of drive the whole time."

Not Tom to Go

When the people have spoken, few ever escape the avalanche that is public opinion. Tom Coughlin did. Barely.

The paying customers at Giants Stadium on December 24, 2006, sought to play the role of judge and jury. Midway through the third quarter, with the Giants trailing 20-7 to the New Orleans Saints, offensive linemen Bob Whitfield and Shaun O'Hara, on consecutive plays, were called for 15-yard unsportsmanlike conduct penalties. Suddenly, for the first time in his three years as head coach of the Giants, a referendum on Coughlin's job status loudly reverberated inside Giants Stadium.

Angry chants of "Fire Coughlin" cascaded down from the seats, descending from all corners of the vast stadium, audible to everyone, surely a dagger into Coughlin's heart.

"I didn't pay attention," he said afterward.

If so, he was the only one.

The jeers did not quiet as the Giants stumbled and bumbled to a lopsided 30-7 loss, making for a Christmas Eve to forget. The Giants went down to defeat for the sixth time in seven games, losing their fourth consecutive home game. So inept were the

Giants that it did not seem plausible that Coughlin could survive the fallout.

Eli Manning, the supposed franchise savior, threw a 55-yard touchdown pass to Plaxico Burress less than three minutes into the game, but after that was 8 for 24 for 19 yards. In the second half, he was 1 for 11 for six yards. The Giants were 0 for 10 on third down, 0 for 1 on fourth down, and did not ever cross the 50-yard line. The Saints ran an astonishing 65 plays in Giants territory.

"I mean, man, you can probably put a high school team out there and get more yards," a flabbergasted Burress said. "I'm just telling the truth."

When Saints running back Deuce McAlister scored with 14:16 remaining to make it 27-7, the fans headed for the exits in droves. This resonated with anyone old enough to recall what team patriarch Wellington Mara always said about the state of his beloved franchise: There is no more disturbing a sight than empty seats.

"We're certainly not proud of what happened today," a shellshocked Coughlin said after the desultory loss. "I feel badly for all Giants fans—on Christmas Eve, to have to lose a game the way this game was lost. One thing that I told the players, it is human nature now, it's very easy to not want to be part of a team that's not having success. The key thing now is for the men to stand up."

The key thing for the organization was to decide whether Coughlin would return for a fourth year or if the fans would get their wish and Coughlin would be sent packing.

The following week, the Giants rose from the wreckage to beat the Redskins in the regular-season finale and squeezed into an NFC Wild Card playoff berth with an unimpressive record of 8-8. They battled but lost, 23-20, to the Eagles in a one-and-done playoff cameo in Philadelphia.

Next came the waiting game, as Giants front-office officials engaged in what was termed "thorough review and discussions." Clearly, the Mara and Tisch families did not want to fire Coughlin, but needed to decide if they could justify his future employment. Three days after the final game, word came down from on high: Coughlin would return and, in order to prevent a lame-duck status, was given a one-year extension on a contract that was due to expire after the 2007 season.

"Tom Coughlin is our coach for 2007 and hopefully for many years after that," team president John Mara proclaimed. "We remain convinced that he is the right man for the job."

The Giants media relations machine pumped out comments from marquee players, expressing relief and satisfaction that Coughlin was safe. This was an opinion shared by some, but certainly not all.

"Guys are so sick of hearing him yapping all the time," said one starting player who asked not to be identified for fear of retribution. "You watch film, a guy gets beat and he yells, 'We can't have that!' Like a whiny baby."

The image of the Giants as dysfunctional, fractured, and undisciplined was not a vision shared by ownership.

"There is this notion out there that [Coughlin] lost the locker room, that there is a mutiny going on down there," Mara said. "That is absolutely not the case."

As for the fans and the "Fire Coughlin" salvo that they offered up to Coughlin as a Christmas present, Mara said he was aware of the discontent, but not stirred to action by it.

"I'm certainly sensitive to what the fans think," Mara said, "but at the end of the day you can't make decisions based on what the fans' sentiments are at that time."

Chapter  5

THE TEAMMATES

No Time for Time-Out

There was one rule linebacker Sam Huff enforced when he was the leader of the Giants defense: We don't call time-outs.

"When you got somebody hurt they would charge you a time-out," Huff said. "One of our players got dinged and four of us picked him up, we wanted to save a time-out for the offense, and we took him to the sideline, he was unconscious, and we threw him in front of the bench."

Sometimes, it was difficult to comply with that rule, but no matter how gory or serious the injury, Huff held firm.

"Another time Dick Modzelewski got his hand stepped on and he was such a great guy, wonderful friend and great player," Huff said. "He comes back to the huddle. He's bleeding like hell and he said, 'Sam, you got to call a time-out, I'm cut.' I said, 'We're not calling time-out, we can't, we got to save 'em.' He said, 'Man, I'm bleeding.'

"A football player does not like to see blood, especially his own. I held his four fingers together, said, 'Hold these four fingers together, I'm going to make this tackle and we're going to get out of here.' I did and we go over to the side, they put four stitches in his hand. But we saved a time-out."

Finding Common Ground

In the late '50s and early '60s, the Giants often were a team divided in that their defense was the dominant unit and viewed itself as the foundation of the franchise. "We used to have our own locker room in training camp," middle linebacker Sam Huff said. "The sign was on the door: Defense Only. We didn't really associate with the offense too much."

At times, members of the defense couldn't resist taking a few shots.

"Allie Sherman used to get mad at us when we hit his stars in practice," cornerback Dick Lynch said. "Don't touch Frank Gifford, Kyle Rote. We never used to let them catch a pass on us if we could help it. We had to let 'em catch it sometimes. Every now and then we wouldn't do it, and he'd get pissed off and yell, 'Goddamn it, what are you doing?'"

The Giants offense often couldn't compete with their more heralded defensive teammates. "You know what, we weren't that bad," Gifford said. "To this day, still, I'll see Sam at a dinner or something and he'll say something. They're just paranoid. I used to play defense, you can't make any money over there. I'd tell 'em that, and it pissed 'em off.

"This really happened. We kept turning the ball over one game, I got back on the field after our defense stopped 'em for the umpteenth time, they got the ball back for us and Sam Huff was going by me and he says, 'Why don't you guys go out and hold 'em for a while?'"

One Tough Guy

He was the quarterback from 1948 to 1961 and he led the Giants in passing for a team-record 12 consecutive seasons and also to the NFL championship in 1956. There were more celebrated signal-callers than Charlie Conerly, but there might not have been any tougher.

"There was a time my rookie year when I really saw it," said Frank Gifford, Conerly's roommate for nine seasons. "He broke his nose really badly, they literally called a time-out and then they called another one while they stopped the bleeding, they stuck stuff up there until it would stop bleeding. You try to get 'em to do that today. They'd be yelling, 'Get my agent!' "

Because of his roots and his experiences for three years as a marine in World War II, "Chuckin' Charlie" took a different view of his profession than most players.

"Charlie was not impressed with football," Gifford said. "He was a down-home country boy from Clarksdale, Mississippi, he had fought in the South Pacific for four years, this was no big deal to him. He had a couple of great years, I'd try to get him to do interviews, I'd say, 'C'mon Charlie, this is *Time* magazine for God sakes.' He'd say, 'I don't give a shit,' and he really didn't. He didn't care about that end of it, he cared enormously about playing. And he was one tough guy."

The Revenge of the Blitz

Cornerback Dick Lynch figured he would be able to coast to the finish of an eventual 48-14 whipping of the 49ers at Giants Stadium on November 17, 1963. Lynch figured wrong.

He did not factor in the wrath of a teammate.

Andy Robustelli not only started at defensive end but he also called the shots as the defensive coordinator. The Giants had this game well in hand and certainly did not need to continue to bring the heat on San Francisco. But they did.

"Andy disliked the 49ers head coach, Jack Christiansen," Lynch said. "We're winning like 30-6 or whatever the hell it was, and Andy wants to work the blitz. Erich Barnes and I are on the corners and we're like, 'C'mon Andy, we got it made here, why do we got to hug 'em?' When you blitz you got to hug, get up there, you work twice as hard hitting the guy.

"He says, 'Shut up! I'm running this defense.'

"So I go over to the sideline and say to Christiansen, 'Andy don't like you, you know? Another blitz is coming, we're gonna blitz.' He yells at Andy, 'You cocksucker, you Guinea son of a bitch!' Oh boy, that's all Andy had to hear!

"We get back in the huddle. We blitz again. I go back to the sideline and say, 'Jack, what are you doing? We got another blitz coming. You're making him mad.' We made the blitz work, it was a tipped ball, and I said, 'I'm getting this son of a bitch ball if I have to kill myself, because I want to stop this running around.' I go up for it, here comes Erich from the other side, both of us had the same idea, I'm gonna get that ball, we got to stop this. He goes up after the ball, he hits me in the chin with his elbow, and I'm in the hospital for three days with a concussion. I was knocked out, but Erich got the interception and we stopped the blitzing."

Fateful Day

He arrived as a 1955 third-round draft pick out of Penn State, a wonderfully rounded bear of a Renaissance man who crocheted, played the guitar and wrote songs, ate nearly everything in sight, and, as a massive defensive tackle, loved to beat on opposing running backs. Yet Rosey Grier was mostly a gentle giant when he landed in New York and immediately encountered culture shock.

"It wasn't natural for me back then because I came from a very segregated community," Grier said. "I was born in Georgia and black kids went to one school, white kids went to another school. I had my thoughts when I came to the New York Giants because Jim Lee Howell was from Arkansas and Charlie Conerly was from Mississippi, Ray Beck was from Georgia Tech. I came expecting that we were not going to get along because of where we were from. And yet Charlie Conerly and I became very good friends. I was close to Jim Lee Howell. I love all those guys. Kyle Rote from SMU took me under his wing. Even out of pro football some place I was singing, I look up and Charlie is sitting in the audience. We just developed a wonderful relationship. I learned a lot as an athlete and I was disappointed when I was traded from the Giants to the Rams."

Ever the freethinker, Grier never allowed his play on the field, first with the Giants and later as part of the Rams' famed Fearsome Foursome defensive line, to define himself. He left football and ventured into a successful and colorful acting and singing career, all the while maintaining a political awareness. He was set to vote for Richard Nixon for president but changed his mind upon hearing that John F. Kennedy called Martin Luther King Jr. when Dr. King was imprisoned.

Soon enough, Grier began working for Senator Robert Kennedy's presidential campaign. "When Ethel and he were doing something for inner-city kids they invited me to Washington, DC, for this big event," Grier said. "I was amazed they considered me a celebrity. I went to their home and Bobby punched me in the stomach and he ran away and I ran after him and we hung together the whole night. We became like instant friends, first time we met."

Grier was on the campaign trail with Bobby Kennedy just past midnight on June 5, 1968, when Kennedy was shot and killed by Sirhan B. Sirhan in a small kitchen pantry at the Ambassador Hotel in Los Angeles, with Grier torturously close to the historic event.

"It was a shattering moment for me, when I took the gun from Sirhan Sirhan," Grier said. "I pulled [Sirhan's] legs up on the table and all these people were around him, [Olympic gold medal decathlete] Rafer Johnson was on the table trying to question him with a lot of other people around. [Writer] George Plimpton was struggling with the gun so I put my hand over the gun and put my thumb under the trigger so it couldn't fire and I wrenched the gun out of his hand and put it in my pocket.

"It was just a time it seems to me all my hopes and dreams for America were gone, yet lingering in my heart was something—I didn't know what it was right then. I went back to LA and I began to try to figure out who I could get to carry on. I got involved in the campaign with [Hubert] Humphrey but nothing happened; we didn't win that one."

Grier eventually found his calling. He became a minister in 1984 and was instrumental in founding Impact Urban America in San Diego, an organization that combines business and ministry to provide jobs and life skills to inner-city youth.

"Like the political campaigns, first I was afraid to talk," Grier said, "and then I realized my voice for hope for us as American citizens was just as good as anyone else's voice, and I should always speak of the things I believe would help us."

Your Move

They both arrived in 1970, Ron Johnson as a running back who played at mighty Michigan and previously spent one year with the Browns, Bob Tucker as a rookie tight end from little-known Bloomsburg State. There was no apparent reason why the two would strike up a friendship that endures to this day.

Check that. There was one apparent reason: Their shared love of chess.

"If you ask him, he'll say I beat him all the time, if you ask me I'll tell you he beat me all the time," Johnson said. "We still sucker-punch each other. It's been about even."

It all started when on road trips in 1970 Johnson and Tucker would observe teammates Carl "Spider" Lockhart and Doug Van Horn playing chess. Tucker would ask in for the next game and roll through the competition. Same with Johnson. Finally, it seemed logical for Tucker and Johnson to play chess against each other.

"From that day on you couldn't separate us," Johnson said. Johnson's roommate was receiver Rich Houston. "He used to go crazy," Johnson said. "Just start laughing at us, because basically Bob became our third roommate."

Finally, after two years Johnson and Tucker became room-mates and the chess games escalated to all-encompassing levels. "Every day, every free moment was playing chess," Tucker said. "Getting ready for practice, putting your socks on, the chess board is right there, we're making moves. Then we had to go to practice and try to preserve the board, guys would change the pieces, but we knew which pieces were where."

Squeezed in between these daily chess adventures, Johnson found the time to lead the Giants in rushing three times, and Tucker found the time to lead the team in receiving four times.

The games are ongoing. Long after they retired, the two kept up the tradition. Tucker lives in Pennsylvania but works in the New York City area. Johnson lives in New Jersey. They are no lon-ger teammates, but they continue to be chess combatants.

"We still get together once every two or three weeks," Johnson said. "He comes over to my house, we eat dinner, and play chess all night."

Ron Johnson (Photo courtesy of the New York Giants)

The Scrambler

The careful planning all week, the hours upon hours of preparation, all the repetition, it all went out the window when Fran Tarkenton went into his dance routine.

"We would always laugh because Fran would never call whatever we worked on all week," running back Ron Johnson said.

"We would get in the huddle and go, 'Oh shit, what do I do on a 39-sweep?' because we hadn't practiced it. I never played with somebody as shrewd as Fran Tarkenton. He probably had limited physical talents, he wasn't tall, didn't have a strong arm, but he was a brilliant tactician, he knew how to move a football team."

From 1967 to 1971, Tarkenton threw 103 touchdown passes and 72 interceptions. In those five seasons the Giants won 33 games and lost 37. It was an inglorious slice of Giants history, but anyone who witnessed Tarkenton play quarterback came away exhausted and usually exhilarated.

"Your job as a receiver was to complement what he's doing," tight end Bob Tucker said. "He would go this way, that way, when your pattern fell apart after the first three or four seconds, you had to just find an open area and do what you can to get open. Finally I learned when I went out to the right and Fran was coming to the right and then he'd stop and go back to the left, I learned I might as well stay where I am, because he'll be back."

Tarkenton came to the Giants from the Vikings and finished his Hall of Fame career back in Minnesota before becoming a wealthy entrepreneur who completely lost touch with many of his former teammates.

"Fran is a master at inspiring people," Johnson said. "I haven't talked to Fran since he left here, he knows how to keep moving on. He made me important in his life when we were together and we had a relationship, but Fran has gone on and done eight zillion other things, some good, some bad, and I understand that's Fran Tarkenton. If we were involved again he would give me 110 percent. He always is trying to maximize Fran Tarkenton, so God bless him."

Good Combo

Billy Taylor, a running back out of Texas Tech, was drafted by the Giants in 1978, and the next year, a big, strong, blond-haired quarterback named Phil Simms arrived as the first-round draft pick. An immediate impression was formulated.

"I thought he was going to be great, it's just that Simms threw the ball too damn hard," Taylor said. "Poor Earnest Gray, I know he broke two or three fingers, Johnny Perkins broke a couple of fingers. Phil really didn't know how to ease up on the ball, didn't have the touch back then. He came out of Morehead State, not a Division I school, I don't think he realized the touch it took. I think he just wanted to show he was strong and brawn."

Taylor loved to catch the ball out of the backfield, and he learned soon enough to keep his hands and fingers ready at all times to avoid getting whacked by one of Simms' fastballs. Other than the occasional soreness, Taylor loved working with Simms.

"He and I developed a relationship right away," Taylor said, "because, to be honest with you, he couldn't read the defenses very well, so he'd always tell me, 'Be ready.' I think that year I had my best year catching the ball."

Sing for Your Supper

It's one of the oldest, silliest, and beloved traditions in football. A rookie comes in, he must sing his school's fight song during a meal in his first training camp. Almost always, the rookie—sheepishly, embarrassingly, proudly, or a combination of all three—gets up and belts out a tune. Sometimes, the guy can even carry a tune.

Sometimes, though, what starts out as a harmless bit of playfulness deteriorates into a situation that's no laughing matter. When Jeremy Shockey was a rookie in 2002 he refused to sing until he finished eating, triggering hostile reactions that led to a dining hall brawl with linebacker Brandon Short.

What transpired back in 1983 didn't quite sink to that level, but it came close.

"Harry Carson and I, early on in our careers, we could intimidate rookies pretty easily, because of our status and our positions and so forth," defensive end George Martin said. "Toward the latter part of our careers these rookies were getting pretty brazen, they were coming in, there were some pretty big boys.

"I remember when Leonard Marshall came in, Leonard at that time was pretty phenomenal for his size. I remember Harry asking Leonard, which is tradition and customary, to stand up and sing his school fight song. Leonard absolutely refused.

"Here it is, this is the moment of truth, Harry's the all-pro linebacker, certainly a team leader, asking this rookie to sing his fight song and the rookie refusing. It's funny, because Harry didn't challenge him. Harry sort of went behind Bill Parcells and said, 'Hey listen, Bill Parcells wants you to sing your fight song.'

"Anyway, Harry then came up behind Leonard and dumped an entire bowl of cottage cheese over his head. Leonard lights out after him, starts running after him, Harry runs behind Bill Parcells, as if Parcells is gonna protect him. Cooler heads prevailed."

Block the Guy!

There is a long list of players who learned, often with much pain and suffering involved, that there was absolutely, positively no way Lawrence Taylor could be dealt with in the usual fashion. Most linebackers can be blocked or at least impeded by a running back on his way out of the backfield. Taylor was not most linebackers. The first NFL back to receive that education was Billy Taylor.

Entering his fourth and last season with the Giants in 1981, Taylor had led the team in rushing in both 1979 and 1980. He admits he was not a devastating blocker, but he was usually athletic enough to prevent opposing linebackers from having their way in the offensive backfield.

But in the summer of 1981, Billy Taylor met Lawrence Taylor, BT vs. LT, and the results were not pretty.

"The running back's job coming out of the backfield before you go out in your pass pattern was to check the linebacker," Taylor said. "So when LT came to camp I could not block him. I remember [coach Ray] Perkins and everybody yelling at me, 'Block the guy!' Yelling, screaming at me, and I'm really trying my hardest, but I couldn't block him. He had too much quickness, more quickness than any linebacker I'd ever blocked against.

"The linebacker doesn't know the plays, so usually I could get up there quick enough to either cut him or get in his face. Either way, he was quicker than me every single time. He either ran me over, ran around me, ran through me, it was almost impossible. I remember feeling bad, I really did, but then later on it came to fruition that nobody else could do it either."

Heavy Lifting

As a veteran of six years in the NFL, defensive end George Martin by 1981 wasn't shocked or amazed by much. Then Lawrence Taylor arrived.

"You couldn't even draw a map for Lawrence for him to find where the weight room was," Martin said. "Lawrence was just a phenom. After the first morning double session everyone would go to their room and pass out, out of exhaustion, he would go to the golf course and play a round of golf.

"One year he came in during the early part of training camp, we had just reported, and we had known Lawrence had had one of those famous Lawrence Taylor offseasons golfing, carousing and partying, and, as he said, the rest of the time he was enjoying himself. He came in and we saw him snatch, without ever lifting a weight, 315 pounds from a dead lift over his shoulders. That had never been done before. Never. When Lawrence did that, you could have heard a rat piss on cotton. I mean, it was astonishing."

Mugging for the Camera

The game is already etched in Giants lore. There was a stunning comeback from a 17-0 halftime deficit. There was the highlight film catch-and-run by tight end Mark Bavaro, who broke four tackles and carried three 49ers defenders on a 31-yard rumble. There were the Giants rallying for a 21-17 victory over the 49ers at Candlestick Park on December 1, 1986, in yet another *Monday Night Football* classic between the two powerhouse teams of the '80s.

For Phil Simms, something else about that famous game is burned into his memory.

"I throw a long pass to Stacy Robinson down the right side to make it 17-14," Simms said, "and I raise my hands up and all of a sudden I feel somebody jump on my back."

That somebody was Billy Ard, the Giants' starting left guard.

"I'm stumbling, he almost knocks me over and I look and I go, 'Billy!'" Simms said. "Billy wasn't one to celebrate like that and go, 'Yeah, man, yeah, yeah!' This is what goes through my head, I go, 'Man, we are so into it, it's even got Billy Ard excited.'

"After the game we're waiting to get on the plane, there's a long line, everybody's trying to get on at once, and he's standing next to me and I say, 'Man, Billy, that was awesome, you were fired up about the game.' He goes, 'Ah, bull.' He goes, 'Phil, it was *Monday Night Football*, you just threw a touchdown pass, I knew the camera was going to be on you, so I just figured I'm gonna jump on you so I can get on TV.'

"It is true, that was why. I said, 'Wow, you just really ruined a great moment.' "

Anything You Can Do . . .

One starred on defense, one ran the show on offense, and both were so competitive that on occasion they couldn't help but test their skills against each other.

"Phil Simms and I used to get into arguments over who could do the other's job better," Lawrence Taylor said. "I said to him one day, 'I can throw this football farther than your ass could ever throw it.' He said, 'Give me a break.'

"I promptly threw that son of a bitch from the 50-yard line into the second level at Giants Stadium. Phil didn't even bother trying once he saw that. 'Take that shit, Simms,' I gloated. Sometimes after practice I'd challenge him to throw the ball into one of those Meadowlands trashcans at least 50 yards away 10 times. He took some money from me on that one."

Taylor retired following the 1993 season, walking away on his own terms, sure he had given everything he had to give. Simms' exit came four months later but, rather than call it quits, he was forced out, released by the team.

"No one expected it, least of all him, because it was like a forced retirement," Taylor said. "Because they don't want you to go nowhere else, but yet they don't want to pay you the big money. That was basically what I had to go through, but I had had it anyway, so that didn't make a difference. But Phil had more to give. I didn't like the idea of them forcing Phil out.

"I remember he thought about playing for Bill Belichick in Cleveland, and I was glad he didn't go and play for another team.

Let me tell you something: Phil Simms, he could have been one of the top five quarterbacks for another two or three years. I didn't understand why they got down on Phil. And where's Dave Brown now? Phil Simms still had several more years of good football left, salary cap or no salary cap. And then another three or four if he wanted to be a backup."

Life with Brad

You get to know someone rather intimately when you work inches apart for seven consecutive years. It's the kind of proximity and familiarity that breeds either friendship or contempt and, sometimes, a little of both.

Billy Ard and Brad Benson were a tandem on the left side of the Giants' offensive line for so long that one might as well have said "Bless you" before the other one sneezed. Ard was the left guard, Benson was the left tackle, and the duo helped anchor an offensive line that protected Phil Simms, blocked the way clear for Joe Morris and helped the Giants to their first Super Bowl triumph.

Along the way, Ard took delight in chronicling Benson's moves and moods.

Benson got yelled at by Bill Parcells early, often, and repeatedly. "Every single day," Ard said. "Bill yelled at guys he knew he could yell at. He would yell at me once and that would shake me up for six months. So if he got after me once a year, that was a lot. He knew I toed the line. Not that Brad didn't, but he's the type of guy you just wanted to yell at. Parcells used to ride him hard all the time, and every single day Brad would come into the locker room after practice and say, 'Fucking Parcells, I'm tired of him, next time he says something I'm gonna let him have it.'

"So one day Brad comes out of practice on a Friday. 'Did you see what Parcells did out there?' I said, 'Brad, he didn't yell at you today.' He said, 'I know he didn't.' He was upset that Bill did not yell at him, he thinks Bill is writing him off because he didn't yell at him, because Bill used to say all the time, 'Hey, if I'm yelling at you all the time you're lucky, because that means you're still here. When I stop yelling at you that means you're gone.' Brad was all nervous because Bill did not yell at him."

Yelling was not the harshest treatment Parcells inflicted on Benson. One day, he almost tried to assault him.

"In 1986 we're in Minnesota, it's the game with the famous fourth-and-17 play, right before the half we're driving in the two-minute drill," receiver Phil McConkey said. "We're trying to get a field goal, we're inside their side of the 50, and Brad Benson has a false-start penalty, which basically takes us out of field goal range.

"The gun sounds, Parcells runs out on the field, he was attacking, he was going after Brad Benson, it was George Martin who had to hold him back. He was livid, absolutely livid. I actually chuckled. It's a scary thing when your coach is going after one of your teammates, but it was humorous."

Old Yeller

The time before the start of football practice can be quiet time, with a few players stretching over here, a few hanging out or tossing the ball around over there. That calm was shattered one afternoon in 1988 by the shrill voice of Bill Parcells. The object of his wrath was none other than quarterback Phil Simms, who had no reason to believe he was guilty of anything.

"It was a cold, cold windy practice inside Giants Stadium," receiver Phil McConkey recalled. "Of course I'm out early catching punts, Parcells is standing right next to me, and Simms is over on the sidelines, screwing around. It's not even stretch time yet, guys are just moseying out.

"Bill said, 'Look at him, look at him, you'd think he'd know better? He's a professional, he should be out warming up, he's over there playing grab-ass.' He says, 'Watch this, McConkey, I'm going to get his ass.'

"So he starts screaming at the top of his lungs, 'Simms, what in the fuck are you doing over there? You dumb-ass, you should be warming up, how can you be playing grab-ass, it's cold out, warm up!' Simms just starts gyrating, gets all nervous, he's looking for his helmet, but somebody hid it in the garbage can, he's scurrying around and Parcells is staying on his ass and I'm on the floor, I'm bent over in laughter, and Parcells is loving it and continuing it to my benefit. I was the only one in on it. Everybody got ramrod straight because they thought he was on a tirade, but he was having fun."

Sweet Revenge

Lionel Manuel remembers exactly where the Giants took him in the 1984 NFL Draft: "Seventh-round, 171st pick. I was scared to death."

Despite playing only one year at receiver in college at Pacific, Manuel found his way onto the Giants roster and as a rookie caught 33 passes. The next season, he led the team in receptions with 49. Yet it wasn't until his third year in the league that Manuel experienced something he'd rather not have encountered.

"That was my first cheap shot," Manuel recalled. "Mr. Antonio Gibson—I'll never forget that name in the world. I'm gonna take that to my deathbed, that name."

In the fourth game on the 1986 schedule, the Saints paid a visit to Giants Stadium. Manuel had no reason to believe this would be the last time he played in the regular season.

"I ran a crossing route in the end zone, the ball went through me, and I was in the process of breaking down. The play was over, whistle blown," Manuel said. "Gibson just decided to go through my knee. Once I got to the locker room, lo and behold, [tight end Mark] Bavaro is sitting in there. The series before Gibson had broken Bavaro's jaw. Same knucklehead. He was a dirty player."

What Manuel considered a classless play unquestionably was a costly one, as he suffered a sprained knee and missed the next 12 games. He was finally able to return for the second playoff game, against the Redskins in the NFC Championship Game, played at Giants Stadium amid a stiff and consistent 35-mph wind.

Sitting out for so long caused Manuel to battle a natural concern as he wondered if his knee could withstand the pounding. "I was really focusing on just catching the football and thinking somebody please hit me," Manuel said. "I just wanted to get that out of the way."

With the Giants leading 3-0 in the first quarter, Redskins head coach Joe Gibbs opted to accept a 10-yard holding penalty on Giants center Bart Oates. Instead of having kicker Raul Allegre trot out to attempt a 43-yard field goal, the Giants were granted another chance on third-and-20 on the Redskins 36-yard line. Simms, out of the shotgun, found Manuel for 25 yards, with Manuel making a fingertip grab in front of cornerback Vernon Dean.

It was Manuel's first catch since the Week 4 hit by Gibson.

On third down from the Washington 11, Manuel was bumped by cornerback Darrell Green, found a hole in the Redskins zone on a crossing pattern, and, with 5:32 remaining in the first quarter, hauled in an 11-yard touchdown pass from Simms.

"I remember just wrapping my whole body around that ball," Manuel said.

The Giants went on to win 17-0 and two weeks later rolled past the Broncos 39-20 in Super Bowl XXI.

These were magic moments for Manuel, but the skinny 178-pound receiver never forgot what Gibson did to him and swore revenge on the 204-pound safety.

"I just wanted to turn the tables, but I never caught up with him," Manuel said.

Down in New Orleans on November 22 of the 1987 season, the Giants ended up losing 23-14 to the Saints, but Bavaro made sure that the thirst for vengeance was satiated.

"Put it this way: Gibson came out at halftime with a cast on his arm," Manuel said. "Bavaro got him before I did. Tit for tat sometimes."

Manuel went into the game determined to make Gibson pay. "Some guys, you get 'em out of the game," Manuel said. "That next year Bill [Parcells] knew the fire was in my eyes, he knew I was gonna get him. I was willing to take a 15-yard penalty, but I was gonna get him.

"Gibson kept staying away from me. Every time I got out there I'm eyeballing him, I'm not even half-thinking about the plays. I waited for him before the game started when they came out of the tunnel. I was trying to eyeball him, and the fans were taunting me, 'Manuel, Manuel, Antonio's gonna get you.'

"All of a sudden he wasn't there any more and I asked Mark about it. He said, 'Don't worry about it' and winked at me. He broke Gibson's arm."

Busted

You think life as an NFL kicker or punter is easy? Try looking busy when you really aren't.

That was the challenge presented to Brad Daluiso, David Treadwell, and Mike Horan when all three were teammates with the Giants in 1993 and 1994. The kicking trio hung out together and, at times during practice, stretched their imagination figuring out ways to appear as if they were actually doing something.

"When it was cold, kickers would always go inside," Daluiso said. "We always did get our work done, and I think I certainly was never unfit, but the reality of it is you can't kick all day and you can't go lift weights all day. There was a lot of downtime, especially when it would get cold.

"Our teammates knew it was pointless to have us standing out there getting pneumonia just so we could be part of the team. So we would go inside and occasionally we might play a hand of cards while practice was going on.

"I remember Horan and I sitting there, we're playing gin and the double doors burst open. We never wanted to be seen playing cards in front of the head coach. The doors burst open, and we are just busted. It's Dan Reeves, he looks right at us, we have our uniforms on, shoulder pads on, we're playing cards. We figure we're fined, we're cut, we're dead.

"He walks right past us, doesn't say a word, goes to the rest room, comes right back out, we're just waiting for it. He looks at us and says, 'What are you playing?' We said, 'Gin.' He looks at us and says, 'God, it's cold out there.' We say, 'Yeah Coach, it is cold out there.' And he heads back to the door and walks out and I thought, 'That was just such a cool thing to do.' "

You Talkin' to Me?

In his eight years with the Giants, Brad Daluiso was the sort of likeable kicker who endures the test of time, consistent on the field and popular off it. He was probably the last player anyone anticipated getting embroiled in an altercation. But he nearly did.

It happened back in 1997 when Daluiso was entrenched as the placekicker as he welcomed in a new punter, a highly touted rookie named Brad Maynard. It is rare when an NFL team uses any of its draft picks on a punter. It is even more unusual when a team, as the Giants did, uses a third-round selection on a punter.

Well, Maynard did not get off to a flying start, and that's where Daluiso nearly bit off more than he could chew.

"I remember Jessie Armstead giving Maynard a hard time one time when Maynard was a rookie, and I spoke up and said something to Jessie," Daluiso said. "We had played together a long time by the time Maynard had gotten there, and I remember saying something to the effect of, 'Hey Jessie, he's young, he's doing the best he can, maybe you ought to lighten up on him a little bit.' I may not have said, 'Lighten up on him a little.' I may have said, 'Maybe you ought to get off his ass, or quit giving him shit.'

Armstead, a Pro Bowl linebacker and unquestioned team leader, was a fierce competitor who was not accustomed to any backtalk from anyone, much less a kicker.

"It was amazing how quickly Jessie went from having that conversation with Maynard to being right up in my face," Daluiso said. "I thought to myself, 'I have Jessie Armstead walking at me with a purpose, oh my God, what have I done?' I was about to die in my own locker room at the hands of one of the best linebackers in football.

"Jessie said to me, 'Daluiso, if I want to talk to you, I'll come up and talk to you.' He basically said until that time, keep your mouth shut. I thought, 'That's probably not a bad idea. That's a good idea, Jessie.' He definitely made his point."

Bat Men

As the Giants surged to the Super Bowl during the 2000 season, they beat up on their division rivals, the Eagles, three times, rushing for 167, 152, and 112 yards. Often, the Giants did nothing other than ram the ball down the throat of the Philadelphia defense. Fancy? No. Effective? Yes.

Amusing? Sure.

"We have this one play, 32, 33 swim, it's double-teams at the point of attack," guard Glenn Parker said. "They know it's coming. At one point in the drive against the Eagles, we're beating 'em, we've used the play already probably 10 times.

"When we got to the sidelines I said, 'Hey, are we going to run a lot more swim?' and everybody just kind of started laughing. I looked at Coach Fassel and said, 'Why don't you just hand us baseball bats and tell us to go hit 'em with them? Give us baseball bats, give them baseball bats and have us hit each other, because this is ridiculous.'

"So we get out there, were in the huddle and he called it again and I said, 'Jesus Christ.' I went up to the line, got in my stance, Kerry Collins was in the middle of his cadence, 'Blue 15, blue 15' and he stopped and said, 'Hey Parks, break out the baseball bats,' and he got right back into his cadence. I started laughing and [center] Dusty Zeigler could barely hold himself."

Non-Grumpy Old Men

Too old. That was the knock on Lomas Brown and Glenn Parker when the Giants acquired the two veteran offensive linemen and immediately inserted them into the starting lineup for the 2000 season. Brown at left tackle was 37 and entering his 16th NFL season. Parker at left guard was 34 and in his 11th year in the league.

Not only did that aged duo survive, the Giants thrived with them anchoring the left side of the line. The two added personality, perspective, and a sense of adventure. When the Giants put the finishing touches on their rousing 41-0 demolition of the Vikings in the NFC Championship Game, Brown and Parker were noticeably moved.

"We were on the sidelines, it was winding down, he came over, we looked at the fans and we just gave this *Dating Game* kiss, bent, turned around backwards, and went over to 'em," Parker said. "Lomas was like a kid in a candy store, having never had the opportunity to ever get to a Super Bowl before. The emotion was so high for all of us, because it was so unexpected."

Two weeks later, the journey did not end happily, as the Giants were routed by the Ravens 34-7 in Super Bowl XXXV. No *Dating Game* kisses this time around.

"Lomas and I took a lot of pride, and I remember looking at him at the start of the fourth quarter," Parker said. "We're down by a large margin, I said to him, 'Hey, don't show it, let's sprint to the ball every time,' and we sprinted onto the field, sprinted to the ball, and we played right to the last moment to the last play because we both realized you don't get many chances like this. We weren't going to have anybody say we didn't give it our best."

When Stars Collide

A team is comprised of 53 players from a variety of backgrounds; no one will ever contend that the disparate personalities always mesh to create a convivial workplace. Rarely, though, does open hostility erupt the way it did during the tumultuous offseason of 2002.

Two of the Giants' most glib, engaging athletes, true marquee players, defensive end Michael Strahan and running back Tiki Barber, engaged in a stunning war of words that shocked their teammates and threatened to rip apart the core of the team.

There is an unwritten rule that players do not comment on the financial dealings and demands of their peers, a rule that Barber willingly ignored when he ripped Strahan for turning down a seven-year, $58-million contract extension. The deal included a signing bonus of $17 million, split between the 2002 season ($10 million) and 2003 ($7 million).

"I don't know if he realizes how much $17 million is," Barber told the *New York Post.* "That is absolutely ridiculous, to turn that down. He's already the highest-paid defensive player in the league. You're telling me that's not good enough for two years? Give me a break."

Barber, who signed a six-year, $25-million deal in 2001 following Super Bowl XXXV, saw himself as coming to the defense of the Giants organization and speaking out against the perception that all professional athletes are greedy.

"We get a bad rap as athletes wanting money all the time," Barber said. "Michael is typifying that when he just should be quiet."

Strahan—coming off a record-setting 22.5-sack season—turned down the gargantuan offer because he feared the split bonus meant the Giants could cut him after one year and he'd never get the $7 million portion of the bonus. Strahan, with one year left on his contract, told *CBS Sportsline* that the 2002 season would be his last one with the Giants and warned his teammates thusly: "The next time they preach to these young guys about the Giants family, I hope they don't buy into that family issue."

The battle lines were drawn. Keith Hamilton, a veteran defensive end, sided with Strahan, ripping Barber in the Newark *Star-Ledger* for being a political puppet of the team. "For him to shoot off his mouth, acting like he's Mr. New York, yes, I'm ticked off about that," Hamilton said.

Privately, members of the front office applauded Barber for expressing what so many within the Giants hierarchy felt but would not say. Upon reading Barber's barbs, Strahan immediately dialed up Barber and engaged in an angry rant, declaring their friendship kaput.

Cooler heads prevailed. Months later, the original deal offered by the Giants no longer on the table, Strahan agreed to a seven-year, $46-million contract. The 2002 season would not be his last one with the Giants.

"I'm glad in this instance I'm the one who looks bad by having the Giants prove me wrong," Strahan said the day he signed.

In training camp that summer, all eyes were on the two during the first team drills, waiting to see if Strahan would get rough with Barber. The day and summer passed without incident. The wounds from this strange affair remained internal.

Shock Value

Maybe it was the headline-grabbing last name or the hard-charging style or the flowing blond hair or the way he captured the imagination of Giants fans salivating at the mere thought of the next Mark Bavaro. Whatever it was, Jeremy Shockey had it, and he made sure everyone knew it. Rarely has a player burst onto the scene—literally—the way Shockey did in the summer of 2002.

A first-round draft pick out of Miami, Shockey's first training camp with the Giants was one for the ages, but not for the faint of heart. He arrived six days late because of protracted contract negotiations and announced his arrival with his fists, engaging in a dining hall brawl with one of his brand-new teammates, linebacker Brandon Short. Shockey proceeded to make headlines and turn heads with some of the most off-color and truly bizarre comments a young player has ever uttered in the early stages of his career.

"All the stuff I say, it's just how I am," explained Shockey, a kid from Ada, Oklahoma, who hit New York by storm and was taken aback when New York hit back.

Shockey's very first practice with the Giants at their training camp in Albany opened a window and let flow this new wind that was about to blow. Short and Shockey engaged in what seemed to be some good-natured trash talk after a pass sailed out of Shockey's reach.

"You look at any great player, they're going to have a fire and some excitement to 'em, and they also have to learn their respect," Short said.

Clearly, pounding respect into Shockey was on Short's mind that night in the team cafeteria. At the time a Giant for two seasons, Short and other veterans approached Shockey and, as per rookie hazing custom, asked him to sing. "After I finish eating," Shockey insisted.

Not good enough. Short heckled and cajoled Shockey as he ate. Finally, Shockey rose to his feet and, in keeping with tradition, stated his name, alma mater, and signing bonus ($5.8 million). Not one to leave well enough alone, Shockey then added, "This is for you, B. Short."

Immediately, Short lunged at Shockey and the two wrestled each other to the floor before head coach Jim Fassel and others served as peacemakers. The Giants at first feared Shockey suffered a concussion, but he had not. He did, though, come away with a bruised cheek and swollen lip.

Fassel's initial reaction was surprisingly supportive of the fracas. "Oh shit man, it was good," Fassel said. "I want guys with energy and feistiness to 'em. I'd rather have to solve those problems than kick 'em in the ass to get 'em going."

On the field, Shockey was just as explosive, surging through a brilliant rookie season with 74 receptions for 894 yards, earning a Pro Bowl selection. Basking in the afterglow of that immediate success, Shockey's second summer with the Giants set new standards for outrageousness. In an interview with *Maxim* magazine, he said many of his new teammates regularly had girls stashed away on the road. He also bashed Cowboys head coach Bill Parcells, calling him "the homo." In other publications, he boasted of binge drinking, multiple sexual partners, and referred to certain women as "hos."

Jeremy Shockey (Photo courtesy of Charles Wenzelberg/NY Post)

Shockey had embarrassed a staid and buttoned-down organization. "You can't take one person's lifestyle and apply it to everyone else," star defensive end Michael Strahan countered.

Tiki Barber, the team's leading running back, said Shockey's remarks "reflect more on Jeremy than this organization."

Enough was enough.

"I want to see this come to an end," an angered Fassel demanded. "He says a lot of stuff tongue-in-cheek. Does that justify it? No. Deep down inside he's not at all what sometimes comes across. He's his worst enemy. You can sit down and talk to Jeremy about anything, and he'll say anything. He's kind of a babe in the woods. I'll have to counsel him and advise him. Forget football, he's too good of a guy to have himself portrayed that way."

Fassel reached out to Shockey's mother, Lucinda, assuring her he'd try to get through to her rambunctious son. In a written statement distributed by the Giants and attributed to Shockey, he supposedly said, "Several of my comments have been thoughtless, immature, and made with a total disregard for those around me. My age is not an excuse and ignorance is not an excuse. My mother taught me better than this."

In an awkward verbal statement orchestrated by the team's media relations department, Shockey said, "The best thing for me to do right now is keep my mouth shut and focus on winning football games." Shockey also issued a warning couched as a prediction: "I am going to be as plain as possible, you'll probably never hear me say an outrageous thing again."

Anyone who believed that ended Shockey's close relationship with controversy was undeniably mistaken. He was eventually traded to New Orleans in July 2008, where he played three years. He retired after a final season with the Carolina Panthers in 2011.

Chapter

THE
CHAMPIONSHIPS

Don't Play, Y.A.

Easy. What else could Sam Huff think?

His first year with the Giants, 1956, was crammed full with glory. Huff was named the league's defensive rookie of the year, and in the NFL Championship Game, the Giants demolished the Bears 47-7. Easy. Huff figured there would be titles galore as his career progressed.

As it turned out, that was it for Huff. In his eight years with the Giants he played in six championship games, but the first was his only ultimate moment of triumph.

Huff's last shot came in 1963 and produced one of his most bitter and heartbreaking memories, as the Giants lost to the Bears 14-10 in the NFL Championship Game in Chicago.

"Larry Morris, a linebacker for the Bears, hit Y.A. Tittle in the left knee and tore Y.A.'s knee up," Huff said. "We were leading 10-7 at that point at halftime. I went into the locker room where they were taping him up and I said to him, 'Y.A., don't play the second half,' because he'd already turned the ball over so many times. It was just not a Y.A. Tittle day, just terrible weather. He liked to throw the ball around. I said, 'We'll win it for you, you got us a three-point lead, that's all we need.'

"I told Y.A., 'You'll wear the ring, just don't do it. We got 'em.' They should have played Gary, whatever the hell his name was, the backup. It didn't make a difference, just don't turn it over, just run three plays and punt, that's all we needed."

Tittle at halftime was injected with pain-killing drugs and pushed back onto the field, even though he clearly was hobbled, as Allie Sherman had no confidence that Glynn Griffing, the rookie backup quarterback, could function. Tittle labored and Ed O'Bradovich intercepted a screen pass that led to Chicago's winning touchdown.

"The old man [Tittle] kept saying, 'I can do it, I feel a little better,'" Sherman explained. "We had a young quarterback [Griffing], he had gone to get married a couple of weeks earlier but failed to come back when he said he would. We couldn't use him." Griffing remained on the bench, Tittle remained on the field. The Giants' lead did not remain for long.

"He wouldn't listen. Allie Sherman played him in the second half." Huff groused, "Y.A. threw another interception. Billy Wade ran the quarterback sneak, and we got beat 14-10."

Off the Mark

He understands why it's called The Greatest Game Ever Played, but pardon Frank Gifford if he refrains from referring to it that way and fails to recall the 1958 NFL Championship Game quite so fondly.

"It certainly wasn't my greatest game I ever played," Gifford said. "It might have been the greatest if you happened to be Johnny

Unitas' mother. If I didn't fumble the ball a couple of times we wouldn't even be talking about it, and if they would have given us the first down we made, you wouldn't be talking about it, either. To a lot of people that was one of the great Giants games. For those of us involved in it, particularly me, it wasn't at all."

Gifford's two fumbles at Yankee Stadium led to 14 second-quarter points for the Colts. Gifford came back to catch a 15-yard touchdown pass from Charlie Conerly for a 17-14 Giants lead early in the fourth quarter.

Then came the moment that Gifford and the Giants view as a great injustice. Late in the fourth quarter, the Giants had the ball on their own 40-yard line, protecting a three-point lead, facing a third-and-four. The call was 47-power, a handoff to Gifford, and he gained the necessary yards for the first down.

Or so he thought.

Baltimore's Gino Marchetti broke his right leg on the play when his teammate, Gene "Big Daddy" Lipscomb, fell over him in a pileup. Amid the chaos, the Giants swear the officials became confused and spotted the ball incorrectly, setting up fourth down.

"There was no question in my mind that I made it," Gifford said. "[Marchetti] was yelling, he was hurt, we all know he was hurt. In a big pileup like that, there's a whole lot of 'mother fuckers' and 'get your ass off me.' Gino was a friend of mine, he had come from San Francisco and we had known each other out there. I felt bad for him, but I had played football for a lot of years at that time, I didn't even look over to the marker because I knew I had the first down. They just didn't pay attention to what they were doing, they marked it short."

The Giants punted the ball away, Unitas took over on his own 14-yard line with 1:56 remaining in regulation, and the rest is permanently woven into the NFL tapestry. The Colts won 23-17 in overtime on Alan Ameche's one-yard run.

"The second thing that went wrong, Jim Lee Howell chose to punt instead of going again," Gifford said. "The only times we had problems moving the ball was when I fumbled. I think we went on third down with 47-power, we got the first down, they marked it short, we should have come back with it, or taken it the other way, 26-power to the other side. We had a good offensive line, they weren't great but they were pretty good, particularly on short yardage."

As he walked off the field, a disconsolate Gifford didn't feel any better when approached by one of the game officials. "Sam Berry said, 'I got to tell you, I'm really sorry about that, Frank,'" Gifford said. "It was blatantly obvious to everyone."

Title-less Tittle

By nearly all criteria, the trade prior to the 1961 season that sent quarterback Y.A. Tittle from the 49ers to the Giants was an quantitative success. In Tittle's first three years in New York he played in three championship games. Yet there's an aura of unfinished business surrounding Tittle's stay with the Giants, as he lost all three.

"I tried to wash 'em out of my mind," Tittle said.

In his first try, Tittle in 1961 found City Stadium in Green Bay an inhospitable place to visit, as brutal cold contributed to Kyle Rote dropping two sure touchdown passes. That set a harsh tone in the Packers' 37-0 rout of the Giants.

"The first year we were not capable, probably, of beating Green Bay," Tittle said. "We had played 'em earlier and played 'em very close [a 20-17 loss]. In the championship game back in Green Bay it was a frozen field, they had a bruising running attack with Paul Hornung and Jim Taylor, and they just dominated the game, we hardly got the ball and we were embarrassed."

Tittle knew he was in for trouble in the 1962 Championship Game the minute he walked outside and was smacked in the face by howling winds. A capacity crowd of 64,892 braved the cold and gale-force winds at Yankee Stadium and went home disappointed, as the Giants could rarely get their passing attack going in a 16-7 loss to the Packers.

"We had 30-mph wind gales," Tittle said. "Going out to the ballgame, vans had turned over, the wind was blowing cars over. Good Lord, I threw balls where the ball would come back and hit me in the face. It was miserable. We did not run the ball as well as Green Bay, and they just pounded away."

The last shot for Tittle came in 1963. That season, he directed an offensive attack that amassed a league-high 448 points, with Tittle leading the way with 36 touchdown passes, a Giants record. He was named the NFL's Player of the Year. The Giants at 11-3 won the Eastern Conference, the Bears at 11-1-2 won the Western Conference, and the two teams met in the title game at Wrigley Field.

Again, the weather conditions (11 degrees at kickoff) hurt Tittle and the Giants deeply. His scoring pass to Frank Gifford and a Don Chandler field goal gave the Giants a 10-7 halftime lead, but Tittle suffered a knee injury and tossed five interceptions. The Bears won 14-10.

"We should have beaten Chicago," Tittle said. "We were the highest scoring team, but we were a passing team, a sort of wide-open type of offense, but we played on a field that Eskimos couldn't have lived on. It was frozen. It was just unbelievable."

Three chances, three misses, no titles for Tittle.

"I was just jinxed," he said.

The Greatest Loss

Players say it all the time. Don't try to do too much. Play your game, play your position, trust your teammates, stay within your talents, and lean on the plan of attack established by the coaching staff.

Sam Huff still grumbles that he tried to do too much. He knows it cost him. He knows he hurt the Giants.

It was later billed "The Greatest Game Ever Played" and there's no reason to believe it wasn't. The 1958 NFL Championship Game at Yankee Stadium was the first football title settled in overtime. Twelve Hall of Fame players appeared in the game and three Hall of Fame coaches strode the sidelines.

Tied at 17, the Colts and Johnny Unitas embarked on a 13-play, 80-yard drive, climaxed by fullback Alan Ameche's one-yard touchdown plunge for a 23-17 Baltimore victory. Before that game-winning moment was a play that continues to haunt Huff.

"The play I remember the most was when I cheated my defense and tried to help [defensive back] Carl Karilivacz cover Raymond Berry and cheated my position a little bit," Huff said. "Johnny Unitas called an automatic and brought Alan Ameche up the middle, that was the biggest run of the day."

With the middle vacated by Huff's over-aggressiveness, Ameche ran 22 yards to set up his own deciding moment.

"That really was the greatest game ever played, even though we lost," Huff said. "I mean, John Unitas was the difference in the game, Johnny Unitas to Raymond Berry. The one thing we did not know how to do on defense was bump and run with the receivers. If we would have known that, we could have beat 'em, Raymond Berry couldn't have gotten off the line of scrimmage. Still, we had 'em, if the official would have given Frank Gifford that first down. It was a bad call. At the end, well, you got one of the great fullbacks of all time scoring in a short yardage play."

"My Favorite Game"

It is the single most famous play during the run to the first Super Bowl victory in Giants history, the fourth-and-17 pass that Phil Simms completed to Bobby Johnson, the play that steered the

Giants past the Vikings 22-20 in Minneapolis, the play known in
Giants circles simply as "The Pass."

That one play, though, is not the main reason why Simms lifts
that game out and places it on a mantle, cherished above all others.

"It's my favorite game in my career, because it was everything I
always wanted to be as a player," Simms said. "I wanted to be tough,

Phil Simms (Photo courtesy of the New York Giants)

making big throws, immune to pressure, not worried about out-
comes. It was truly like standing on the tee box in golf and there's
trees on each side and water and you just go, 'Man, I'm gonna rip it
down the middle.' And no other thought crosses your mind."

There was so much agony in that game and so much physical
pain and suffering. "I took a beating that no man should ever take,
in any life, that day," Simms said. "Hell, all of 'em, Keith Millard,
George Martins brother [Doug Martin], Joey Browner, man he
clothes-lined me one time, but we made a lot of plays, we were up
and down the field, we never got it in, it was some frustration, but
we just hung in there and kept fighting.

"In the last quarter alone we must have had five chances to
win the game, and we couldn't get it done. The drive when we
got the fourth-and-17, I dropped back and they covered the pass
and I looked to the weakside receiver, which was never taught to
me, and Stacy Robinson was running deep down the right sideline
and I threw a bomb, and when I tell you I threw it perfect, it's an
understatement. He should have caught it and walked into the end
zone. It was Stacy Robinson's first game back, he'd been out with
an injury, and he bobbles it and kicks it and throws it out there
and drops it. I just remember not even thinking anything about it.

"Of course moving down the way we did to score and hitting
fourth-and-17 just makes it a better story."

The Giants trailed 20-19 with 72 seconds remaining inside
the raucous Metrodome, all but dead when Doug Martin sacked
Simms for a nine-yard loss to set up a near-impossible situation:
Fourth down, 17 yards to go from the Giants' 48-yard line. At a
frantic, desperate time, the Giants were neither frantic nor desperate as they huddled on the sideline. Bill Parcells, receivers coach
Pat Hodgson, offensive assistant Ray Handley, backup quarterback
Jeff Rutledge, and Simms all brainstormed, searching for one bolt
of lightning.

They came up with "Half-right 74."

"Everybody was in agreement that the one we finally ended up running would give me three chances to throw the ball down the field to pick up a fourth-and-17," Simms said.

"This is not embellishing the story, I remember right before we broke the huddle I said to Bobby, 'Be alert, if they play the coverage I think they will, there might be a little spot for you on the sideline.' Of course I said that about 8,000 times to receivers in my career. Quarterbacks are a lot like coaches sometimes, they want to tell everybody every little piece of information they have in their mind before they break the huddle."

Simms got the pass off just as defensive tackle Mike Stensrud was about to nail him for a sack. Simms, knocked down, never saw what happened next.

"I just get it off, I think I get over [cornerback] Issiac Holt's fingertips by an inch, I knew it was going to be close, but the thrower always knows. I knew they were almost going to knock it down, but I knew they wouldn't. You can always tell when it leaves your hand. It's a pretty neat feeling."

"The Pass" went for 22 yards. Five plays later, Raul Allegre with 12 seconds left kicked his fifth field goal of the game, the Giants were winners, and Simms had his favorite game ever.

Dress for Success

Something was wrong. George Martin could feel it. The veteran defensive end knew how the locker room should look and feel prior to a playoff game, and Martin didn't see or sense the proper urgency or focus from his teammates.

It was a cold and windy January 4, 1987, as the Giants readied themselves to face the 49ers in an NFC semifinal game at Giants

Stadium. Martin looked around and was dismayed as the hours before kickoff more closely resembled a department store fitting room than an NFL locker room.

"There was, not really a controversy, but a huge discussion in the locker room prior to us coming out for warm-ups as to what we were gonna wear," Martin said. "Guys are saying, 'Let's get these kind of shoes. Are you gonna wear your long johns? Are you gonna wear long sleeves or short sleeves?' I mean, it was like a fashion show. Everyone wanted to be comfortable and warm. That's where our focus was."

Before Martin could speak up and redirect the thoughts of the Giants, a certain middle linebacker, in a stunning display of muted eloquence, served notice that clothes do not make the man.

"In the midst of this discussion, I kid you not, Harry Carson walks from the training room on the northern end of the locker room to his locker all the way on the very southern end," Martin said. "He didn't say a word, he walked through fully dressed, with no sleeves, cutoff jersey cut at the waist, he was showing his abdomen, and he had a cutoff T-shirt.

"This man walked passed us like he was on his way to an execution and he was the executioner. He didn't say a word and everybody looked at him and to a man, everybody threw all of those long johns, all of the sleeves away, and the rest, as they say is history. We went out there, under his sign of leadership, and won 49-3. Our focus, in an instant, changed, and had he not done that, the outcome would have assuredly been different."

What a Call

By the end, the Giants' 39-20 triumph in Super Bowl XXI was indeed a rout, but tucked inside that defeat of the Broncos was a tight, taut game for more than one half. And included within the pressure of the moment was a bold move by Bill Parcells that helped turn a Giants deficit into a lead they would never relinquish.

"I think in that game Bill Parcells made one of the great calls in Super Bowl history, and no one ever talks about it," guard Billy Ard said.

Here's the deal: The Giants, trailing 10-9, took the opening kickoff of the second half to their own 46-yard line and faced a fourth-and-one. Clearly, most coaches would have punted the ball away, fearful that failure to pick up the first down would hand John Elway the ball, already inside Giants territory. Parcells eschewed a punt and instead dusted off a trick play.

The Giants called it "The Arapahoe," named for the Native American tribe.

"Romeo Crennel came up with the idea," Ard said. "It was our fake punt. We bring our punt team on the field and then we change, Jeff Rutledge would go to quarterback and we had three plays we could run. We ran it against Denver earlier in the season. We had a play called Flow 36, which was a sweep to the right, we had some other play, and then we had a thing called Roll Tide, because Jeff Rutledge went to Alabama, so Roll Tide meant quarterback sneak.

"Jeff's standing over the center, he's saying, 'Are you sure you want me to snap it, are you sure you want me to snap it?' Parcells goes, 'Snap it.' I remember the Denver linebacker, Karl Mecklenburg is like, 'We know where you're going.'

"Jeff had choices, he could have done anything he wanted. Roll Tide, he went with the quarterback sneak and got the first down. We rolled and won it. It's like a great call in the Super Bowl and no one talks about it."

Rutledge picked up two yards and the first down, and the Giants went on to score a touchdown on a Phil Simms pass to Mark Bavaro.

The Final Gun

There is much Phil McConkey can take pride in about his contributions in the Giants' 39-20 Super Bowl victory over the Broncos. After all, he set up a field goal with a 25-yard punt return, he set up a touchdown with a 44-yard catch off a flea-flicker, and he scored a touchdown on a six-yard reception, grabbing a deflected pass in the end zone off teammate Mark Bavaro.

Great memories, all, but what happened after the game is even more indelible. Amid the uproar of the postgame celebration, McConkey spotted a handgun on the field.

"The game's over, I'm ecstatic, jumping up and down, there's a ton of people on the field," McConkey said. "If you went and got the game tape from CBS, the camera's on Phil Simms following him off the field and you can see me like a madman run by with a helmet in my one hand, the next shot shows me with the helmet in my one hand and a gun in the other hand and a security guard taking it from me.

"The CBS switchboard was getting calls that I had a gun. Security said one of the security guys was wrestling with a fan and dropped it. At the press conference afterward somebody asked me about that and I said, 'Yeah, I scored a touchdown today at the Super Bowl, and I saved some lives by picking up a gun.' Just surreal. Talk about something not belonging there."

Almost Perfect

As he geared up for the biggest game of his life, Phil Simms felt two disparate emotions surging through his body. One was supreme confidence. The other was complete disregard for the consequences of failure.

In the days leading up to Super Bowl XXI in Pasadena, California, Simms was unusually calm. This was the first Super Bowl for Simms, the first for the Giants franchise, yet the upcoming game against the Broncos was viewed less as an obstacle and more as an opportunity.

"During practice the look Bill [Parcells] and I would give each other, I think it was a look that he was trusting me and I trusted him, and the fact I was not going to let anything get in the way of the game," Simms said. "The bigness of the game was not going to be a hindrance to my performance. I was ready to go down in flames, I was prepared to do that, I was not worried about having a bad game and being hung or run out of New Jersey or New York or whatever.

"I didn't think about it, I just played."

How he played. No quarterback in Super Bowl history played the way Simms did that January 25, 1987, when he staged a near-perfect exhibition on lush Rose Bowl grass. He completed 22 of 25 passes for 268 yards, three touchdowns, and no interceptions. He set Super Bowl records (10 consecutive completions, connecting on 88 percent of his passes). The Giants overwhelmed Denver with 30 second-half points en route to a 39-20 victory. Simms won the Most Valuable Player award.

"You can't play any better than that," Parcells said.

"For myself, until I saw my numbers up on the board I went, 'Wow, 22 of 25, wow, really, that's pretty cool,' and then I just went, 'Damn, I don't remember throwing any incomplete passes.' It was the first time it really crossed my mind."

Work of Art

Prior to kickoff for Super Bowl XXI in Pasadena, California, Billy Ard took his customary place far off to the side as the Giants lined up for the national anthem. As the starting left guard, Ard was about to play in the most important game of his life and he sought a final moment of solitude.

Just then, he spotted someone who usually wasn't stationed on the sideline.

"I see Leroy Neiman right next to me," Ard said. "He has this big handlebar mustache, he's a very easy guy to recognize, and I say to him, 'Hey, you're Leroy Neiman!' He looks at me and goes, 'Yeah.'"

This unexpected brush with a pop artist, who happened to be a fixture at Super Bowls, combined with the tension of the day left Ard feeling just a bit giddy. Neiman was on hand to chronicle the big game in his own special way, to paint a lasting remembrance, saluting the victors.

Ard figured he had nothing to lose.

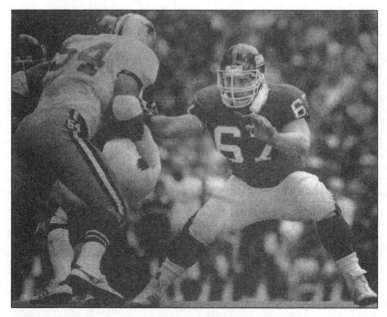

Billy Ard (Photo courtesy of the New York Giants)

"I'm like, 'Hey, put me in your picture, put me in your painting,'" Ard said. "I knew he always painted the offensive team. He said, 'You got to win that game,' and I said to him, 'We will win that game.' No lie."

Indeed, Ard's words proved to be prophetic, as the Giants beat the Broncos 39-20. Ard never gave his brief conversation with Neiman a second thought.

And then . . .

"About two or three months later I get a phone call from a woman who owns an art gallery," Ard said. "She says, 'Bill, there's a Leroy Neiman here and you're smack-dab in the middle of it.' So I run on down, I pay like $3,000 for it, I didn't care. What's it cost? Boom, bought it.

"It's a picture of Phil Simms going back, he's getting tackled, it's a typical Neiman-type of picture. It's taken from the right side of the field, Simms is going back, he's opening up to the right side, he had Joe Morris to the right and Karl Nelson to the right, you have Mark Bavaro to the right and you have me right in the middle with the Denver defensive tackle Rulon Jones.

"You know what? I was never on the right side of the ball, never blocking to the right. All I can tell you is Leroy Neiman stuck me right in the middle of that freaking picture because I asked for it. I'm telling you what, he threw me in there, big number 67 in the middle of the picture. It's my pride and joy. That's my Super Bowl moment. I have it hanging up right in the middle of the family room when you walk in, right over the fireplace. Beautiful."

All Wet

The sons were there with their dad, having made the giddy trip down from the press box at the Rose Bowl, entering a quiet locker room a few minutes before a wild celebration would erupt.

There, Wellington Mara and his sons watched on a small television the final moments of the Giants' 39-20 victory over the Broncos in Super Bowl XXI, the first Super Bowl triumph in franchise history.

"After a really painful period in our history, all those years without winning a championship, that was a pretty special memory, something I'll always remember," John Mara said. "The players came in and took my father into the shower."

This was no ordinary dunking. Wellington Mara was not going to get doused without first being ready.

"I don't remember how I knew it, but I knew Harry Carson was going to want to put me in the shower," Wellington Mara said. "So I said, 'Harry, let me take off my shoes and my jacket, will ya?' He said, 'OK, Mr. Mara.' So I took them off and then I went into the shower with him. He was very kind to let me take them off."

Trophy Guy

First as a student intern, then as an assistant trainer, later as the head trainer, and later still as the senior vice president of medical services, Ronnie Barnes taped more ankles and befriended more players than anyone ever associated with the Giants. He was hired by the team in 1976 and more than 40 years later remains a vital and respected cog in the inner workings of the team.

The very nature of the job forces Barnes to restrain his emotional investment in the success or failure that transpires on the field. His must be one of the cooler heads on the scene at all times. Still, special times call for special responses, and Barnes couldn't help himself when the Giants returned home after trouncing the Denver Broncos in Super Bowl XXI in Pasadena.

"The greatest moment for me was when we came back in '86. We drove into the parking lot," Barnes said. "We were a fairly unsophisticated organization. We just took our team down, played, and came back on the bus, and Lot D at Giants Stadium was filled with fans.

"The [Lombardi] trophy was just kind of sitting over on a chair and I grab the trophy, not grandstanding or anything. I'm thinking maybe the fans will want to see it. So I got in the window and held the trophy up. Well the fans started beating on the bus and [Bill] Parcells is sitting there yelling, 'Put the trophy down; they look like bees out there!' "

Mostly, Barnes made his impact in behind-the-scenes fashion as a loyal confidant to countless players. Barnes also forged a unique bond with co-owner and team patriarch Wellington Mara that grew more and more vibrant until the day Mara died—when an 89-year-old New York City Irishman and a 53-year-old black man from Rocky Mount, North Carolina, sadly parted ways.

Mara passed away on October 25, 2005, and four days later the outside world got to know just how close Barnes and Mara grew over the many years. When it came time for the funeral eulogy, John Mara—the oldest of Wellington's 11 children—made sure to acknowledge Barnes before almost anyone else.

"There is one person who deserves special thanks," John Mara said, "Ronnie Barnes, who my mother refers to as her twelfth child. He spent night after night and many days in my father's hospital room, taking such good care of him. 'Is Ronnie coming tonight?' my father would ask. Of course, the answer always was yes, and my father's face would light up when Ronnie walked into the room.

"My father asked him one night, 'Ronnie, why are you so good to me?' 'Because, Mr. Mara, you've always been so good to me,' Ronnie replied. Nobody took better care of him and there is no one he trusted more."

A Bad Break

Few games ended with the sudden, shocking finality of the Giants' 19-13 overtime loss to the Rams in an NFC semifinal play-off game on January 7, 1990. Anyone who was at Giants Stadium that day will never forget the sight of Flipper Anderson barely getting a half-step on cornerback Mark Collins, reaching up and hauling in a 30-yard touchdown pass from Jim Everett. The decisive score was horrific enough to the 76,325 on hand, but seeing Anderson run through the end zone and clear through the tunnel, never breaking stride as he disappeared from view, was the very definition of sudden death for the Giants.

It was a game and a play that Collins, quite understandably, could choose to distance himself from. Yet Collins says, "That was a great game for me, I'll never forget it."

A great game?

"Everyone talks about being in a zone," Collins said. "I was in a zone that game. I had a great interception over Flipper Anderson. I had tackles. I did everything. I had a great game that game until maybe the fourth play of overtime."

That's when Collins glided over to make a tackle on Rams tight end Pete Holohan near the Los Angeles sideline. "I remember hearing my ankle snap," Collins said. "The funny part of it was when I broke my ankle I knew something was wrong. I snapped out of the zone, I said, 'Wait a minute, hey man, I'm hurt.' It was obvious. It's the weirdest feeling."

Collins tapped his hand to his helmet, the acknowledged signal when a player wants out of the action. There was no response from the Giants coaching staff. Bill Belichick, the Giants defensive coordinator, motioned for Collins to play bump-and-run coverage on Anderson, which is a difficult assignment with two sound ankles, a near impossibility when one of the ankles is broken.

"I didn't tell anybody I did this, I kept playing, kept playing," Collins said. "Somebody upstairs with the Rams, I think it was Ernie Zampese, called down to coach [John] Robinson that I was limping. The Rams, being smart as they were, went no-huddle. I got a good jam, I was stride for stride with Flipper Anderson. It was a great throw, a great catch, and that's the end of the story."

Amid the disgust and disappointment, Collins hobbled into the trainer's room, where X-rays confirmed what Collins already knew: He played that final, fateful play with a broken ankle.

"There were about 90 media people at my locker," Collins recalled. "I sat there and I talked, and I never brought it up that my ankle was broken. I answered every question for a good hour. I got up, showered, and I went home. Got on a plane, went to California, and then it came out later that my ankle was broken. A lot of the media called me up at home and asked, 'Why did you not use that as an excuse?' I said, 'It wasn't.' That's why I have a great relationship with the media in New York and New Jersey. I'm a standup guy. I take my lumps."

One reporter went as far as to send Collins a bottle of wine, a gesture of respect to an athlete who refused to make excuses.

"The best thing about it," Collins said, "I came back the next year and shut that guy [Anderson] down and we won the Super Bowl."

The Best Game

As riveting a game as it was, what Bill Parcells remembers most profoundly about the Giants' pulsating 15-13 victory over the 49ers in the NFC Championship Game on January 20, 1991, was a comment long after the cheering had subsided.

In many ways, it was perhaps the greatest achievement in the Parcells era. The 49ers, coming off consecutive Super Bowl triumphs, were going for a Super Bowl three-peat and were favored to do just that, playing at home at Candlestick Park. The Giants, playing with backup quarterback Jeff Hostetler after Phil Simms was lost late in the season to injury, failed to score a touchdown. Yet Matt Bahr's record five field goals, including a 42-yarder at the final gun, provided just enough points for the resilient Giants, who knocked Joe Montana out of the game and down the stretch coaxed a critical fumble out of Roger Craig.

"What I remember about the game the most was said to me by Jerry Markbreit, who to this day will tell you this," Parcells said. "He said, 'I was a referee for 467 games in the National Football League, and that's the greatest game I ever refereed.' He's told me that two or three times, reminded me of it. I told him, 'Jerry, it was only a great game because of the great players playing in it.' They had about 10 and so did we. That's really true. You think about the guys who were there, the Montanas and Lotts and Roger Craigs and Haleys and Lawrence Taylor and our guys, Ottis Anderson, Mark Bavaro and the guys we had. There were some good players on both sides."

The Perfect Plan

After watching the Buffalo Bills dismantle the Dolphins (44-34) and Los Angeles Raiders (51-3) in back-to-back playoff games, members of the Giants defense knew they would be severely challenged in Super Bowl XXV. After all, the mighty Bills and their hyperactive no-huddle offense scored 428 points that season and were averaging 47.5 points in the postseason.

Factoring in everything he possibly could, Giants defensive coordinator Bill Belichick came up with a goal for his unit. "We felt as a defense if we could keep those guys under 20 points we could win," cornerback Mark Collins said.

Easier said than done.

"Bill Belichick said listen, we have to take something away, we take away the passing game, the quick strike, we have a chance to win this game," Collins said. "We knew Thurman was going to get his yards."

That would be Thurman Thomas, who needed only 15 rushing attempts to amass 135 yards. Yet the game plan worked to near-perfection. The Giants were so efficient on offense they hogged the ball for a Super Bowl-record 40 minutes, 33 seconds. The Giants were so physical on defense that the Bills rarely got their fast-break attack moving.

For all the strategizing and hard hits, the key to the defensive plan may have been an unprecedented maneuver by Belichick to combat Buffalo's no-huddle attack. He came up with an ingenious way to convey just how rapidly his defense needed to line up play after play.

"To get us used to the no-huddle offense we actually watched the NBC coverage, the game itself, with Dick Enberg announcing the game," Collins said, "so we could get the time of how much it would take to huddle up, to run a play. Never been done before. Bill Belichick said, 'OK guys, watch this film, let your clock in your mind run to see how much time you got to gather and call a play.' Perfect."

When Scott Norwood sent a 47-yard field goal attempt wide right on the final play of the game, the defensive plan turned out to be perfect and also prophetic. The Giants prevailed, 20-19, to win their second Super Bowl in five years. Yes, indeed, the Giants (barely) held the Bills under 20 points. And they won.

Jessie's Prediction

The victorious coach, Jim Fassel, was standing on a raised platform, behind a lectern, offering up his version of the perfection he just orchestrated when suddenly and somewhat rudely, he was interrupted.

Fassel was basking in the glow of a resounding 41-0 dismantling of the Vikings in the NFC Championship Game following the 2000 season when his postgame press conference was halted by an intrusion. Linebacker Jessie Armstead, unannounced and, at the moment, uninvited, strutted to the front of the room, causing Fassel to pause as all eyes turned to monitor Armstead's unusual maneuver.

Armstead lifted up a corner of the lectern, where a folded piece of paper was lodged. He picked up the scrap, placed the lectern back in place, and then unfurled the paper, revealing the hidden message as if it were buried treasure.

Written on the paper was the following: "Giants 31, Vikings 17."

What was going on here?

"I visualized 31-17," said Armstead, a Pro Bowl linebacker and the heart and soul of the Giants defense.

Earlier that morning, Armstead had put his prediction on paper and quietly stuck it where he knew Fassel's postgame press gathering would take place, expecting to retrieve the evidence several hours later. The show of faith was a stark contrast to the meager expectations for the Giants, who were a 50-1 shot to make the Super Bowl.

The game was never close. Armstead had underestimated his teammates, or perhaps overestimated the Vikings.

"We felt if we held them to 17 points or less, we'd win," Armstead explained. "I never thought we'd shut them out. But we played really well. When we got into the third quarter and they still hadn't scored, we said, 'Let's keep that goose egg.' And we hung on to it."

"My Greatest Thrill"

No single victory, no matter how enthralling, can entirely wipe away the sting of monumental losses, but for general manager

Ernie Accorsi, witnessing the Giants' 41-0 thrashing of the Vikings in the NFC Championship Game following the 2000 season was the next best thing.

"I had lost three championship games, two of 'em in the most excruciatingly painful ways you can lose, you can't lose two games like that," Accorsi said. "I remember before the game against the Vikings, walking out with [announcer John] Madden to Saturday's practice, I couldn't fathom losing another championship game. He said to me losing this game is worse than losing the Super Bowl."

Previously, Accorsi, as general manager of the Browns from 1985 to 1992, watched, first with glee and then disbelief, as Cleveland advanced to three AFC title games and lost them all. Two of the setbacks burn forever in Cleveland lore and are constant irritants stuck in Accorsi's heart, unable to be soothed by the strongest antacid.

In the 1986 AFC title game at Cleveland Stadium, Accorsi watched as his Browns led 20-13 with 5:43 remaining in regulation, with the Broncos pinned back on their own two-yard line. John Elway then engineered "The Drive," a 98-yard masterpiece to tie the score. The Browns lost in overtime 23-20.

The next year in Denver, the Browns surged to 30 second-half points to pull even at 31-31. After another Elway drive put the Broncos up 38-31, Accorsi couldn't believe his eyes when running back Ernest Byner, on the Denver three-yard line and poised to send the game into overtime, fumbled the ball away. The Browns lost 38-33.

With those losses coursing through his veins, Accorsi is unable to relax until a game, no matter how one-sided, is officially over. At halftime of the playoff rout of the Vikings, the Giants were in commanding position, leading 34-0, yet Accorsi's face remained gray, almost ashen. Clearly, he was not yet convinced, refusing to feel safe about anything.

Never one to leave his seat up in the press box prematurely, Accorsi finally relented, as Kerry Collins had already thrown five touchdown passes and the Giants opened up a 41-point lead. Years later, he recalls he made his way down to the soggy grass field at Giants Stadium with 7:41 remaining, the exact time etched in his mind. The capacity crowd, engaging in a joyful end-to-end blowout, was in full, throaty party mode, and Accorsi wasn't going to miss the rare opportunity to bask in the glow of this historic rout.

"It was a surreal experience," Accorsi said. "Those last seven minutes, which probably took about 20, were the greatest seven minutes of my career. You never have a game won in my mind, but standing on that field, having Joe Montgomery pick up first down after first down to get the game over with, to have it happen in New York. Listen, winning the Super Bowl is what you work for. Getting there is also an incredible experience. It was just a fulfilling moment I can't even explain. That would be my greatest thrill."

No Intro Blues

As they had done throughout the 2000 season, fast friends Greg Cornelia and Tiki Barber shared a ride to Giants Stadium prior to the NFC Championship Game. Barber, searching for some inspiring words, remembered that for this game, the Giants defense would be introduced to the crowd, as coach Jim Fassel all season alternated which unit would get to run through the tunnel in the featured spotlight.

"Right before we got into the parking lot," Barber said, "the last words I said to him were, 'The good thing is Greg, if we win this game, we'll get introduced at the Super Bowl.' Just a little pick me up."

Sure enough, the Giants whipped the Vikings 41-0 and Barber, along with his teammates on offense, were anxiously awaiting the fulfillment of a childhood dream.

"I'm a small-town guy from Roanoke, Virginia, all my friends are going to be watching the Super Bowl," Barber said.

Two days before the game, Barber experienced a wholly unexpected letdown. At a team meeting, Fassel stated that the defense, and not the offense, would be introduced at the start of Super Bowl XXXV.

"Because they had more veterans and were the ones that carried us, and he felt it was the right thing to do," Barber said. "It was an enormous letdown for the offense. The defense got introduced instead of the offense, and that killed us. It was a little thing, but he killed it. It was our turn. We've seen it at the Super Bowl since we were 10 years old, 'Now starting at running back, Tiki Barber.' That's what I was imagining, forget national television, this was world television, and Coach Fassel the day before said we were gonna introduce the defense."

The Giants on offense were nearly nonexistent in the game, generating no points in a moribund 34-7 loss to the Ravens. Was the perceived slight during the pregame introduction a reason why?

"Maybe," Barber said, before adding, sarcastically, "The fact we couldn't block, couldn't get a person on Ray Lewis had nothing to do with it."

Best of Times, Worst of Times

It's a question Tiki Barber can't answer, and he was the one who lived through it. "I don't know if it's possible," Barber asked, "to have your best day and your worst day on the same day."

There is no doubt it was an unforgettable day for Barber.

Heading into the final game of the 2002 season, the Giants sat on the brink of playoff inclusion, needing a victory over the Eagles, who at 12-3 had already clinched the NFC East crown. Towels

Tiki Barber (AP Images)

were distributed to fans at Giants Stadium emblazoned with a simple message: Win & In.

The Giants dominated on the field but not on the scoreboard as Barber embarked on one of the most remarkably eventful games any running back has ever assembled. He established career highs for rushing attempts (32) and yards (203). He caught eight passes for 73 yards. His rushing yards and total yards (276) were both the second highest single-game totals in franchise history. Yet three times, he lost the ball on fumbles.

"It was almost like a runner when he has a runner's high, where he feels he's invincible, I felt that way," Barber said. "The game should have been 30-7, but I fumbled three times and stopped drives. The only thing that was stopping me was myself."

Barber's third fumble, at the Giants 26-yard line, prompted him to fling his helmet in disgust. Firmly prepared to admit he had cost his team a shot at the playoffs, Barber braced for the inevitable when Eagles Pro Bowl kicker David Akers with 1:12 remaining in regulation attempted and shockingly missed a 35-yard field goal attempt.

"It's amazing I didn't have a mental breakdown," Barber said.

Spared, the Giants headed into overtime, tied at 7-7, and Barber would have understood if coach Jim Fassel did not trust him with the ball.

"He could have destroyed my confidence as a player by pulling me but he stuck by me," Barber said.

Fassel was rewarded when Barber gained 29 yards on the drive that culminated in Matt Bryant's 39-yard field goal for the 10-7 victory that put the Giants in the playoffs. Barber wept as the ball sailed through the uprights. Afterward, team co-owner Wellington Mara said, "Somewhere, Joe Pisarcik is smiling; he feels vindicated."

And Barber kept his sanity after the best-worst game of his career.

Chapter

MAKING A STAND

Title Turnaround

There did not appear to be anything particularly special about the Giants entering the 2007 season. They were coming off a mundane 8-8 record the previous year, taking the field for the first time in 10 years without retired Tiki Barber, the franchise all-time rushing leader, and seemingly their only major addition was the hiring of a new defensive coordinator, Steve Spagnuolo, who had never before ascended to that role.

The Giants plucked Spagnuolo away from the archrival Eagles, where he was the coach in charge of linebackers and regarded as an assistant who could handle a more prominent and pressure-packed position leading an entire defense. In his first two games with the Giants, Spagnuolo's defense allowed 45 points to the Cowboys at Texas Stadium and 35 more points to the Packers in the home opener at Giants Stadium.

There were lusty boos for the home team, with fans heading for the exits in droves early in the fourth quarter. The Giants fell to 0-2 for the first time in 11 years and allowed 80 points in their first two games, more than any Giants defense since Allie Sherman was running the sinking ship at the start of what became a 1-12-1 season low-lighted by the paying customers singing "Goodbye Allie."

There were no derisive serenades just yet for Tom Coughlin but it was getting late early for the head coach and his first-year defensive coordinator. "I think we're a better football team than we've shown," Coughlin said, before admitting, "Obviously I don't have any real grounds for saying that. It's just a belief."

Star defensive end Michael Strahan, who considered retirement before returning for a 15th year with the Giants, knew trouble when he sensed it. "I've seen worse," Strahan said before warning, "The key thing is, don't panic."

Panic figured to be high on the list of unfortunate options for the 0-2 Giants the following week in front of a record crowd of 90,803 at FedEx Field in Landover, Maryland. "We came in basically telling ourselves we need to win or that's probably the end of our season," defensive end Justin Tuck said.

The end of the season didn't look far off when the Giants lugged a 17-3 deficit into halftime. The Redskins were 30 minutes away from dropping the Giants to 0-3 and perhaps forcing Coughlin and Spagnuolo to start updating their resumes. But after scoring 21 straight points to grab a 24-17 lead, the Giants and Spagnuolo's defense were on the spot as the Redskins were on the march, landing on the Giants one-yard line with 58 seconds remaining in regulation, dangerously close to sending the game into overtime.

There was plenty of time for the Giants to fold. "The only thing we're thinking," linebacker Antonio Pierce said, "is stop them."

The Redskins spiked the ball on first down to stop the clock. Linebacker Kawika Mitchell prevented fullback Mike Sellers from making a catch on second down. On third down, the Giants expected the ball to be run to the right side—away from Strahan. "Where else were they going to go?" asked Osi Umenyiora, the defensive end on the right side. "I was like 'Well, it's now or never.'"

It was now. Ladell Betts was hauled down by Mitchell for no gain. On fourth down, with 25 seconds left and the season staring them in the face, the Giants finished what they started. Betts slipped after getting the ball from quarterback Jason Campbell and went nowhere, plowed under by Tuck, Aaron Ross, James Butler, and perhaps the specters of Sam Huff and Lawrence Taylor. Spagnuolo's defense had come up with a defensive stand to remember, and the Giants avoided a season to forget.

"You can't write a story better than that," marveled Tuck.

"To stop 'em like that, a goal-line stand, greatest feeling in the world," exclaimed Umenyiora.

A season was saved, and a career was energized. The next week, Spagnuolo's defense tied an NFL record with 12 sacks against the Eagles, with Umenyiora getting six of them all by himself. Spagnuolo's unit evolved into a fearsome bunch that carried the Giants to a 10-6 record, into the playoffs and through a remarkable postseason run that did not end until Coughlin was hoisting the Lombardi Trophy after upsetting the Patriots in Super Bowl XLII—fueled by a defensive surge that limited the potent New England offense to 14 points. Spagnuolo, hailed and suddenly in demand, spent one more year directing the Giants defense before attaining his dream of becoming an NFL head coach, entrusted with turning around the moribund St. Louis Rams. That goal-line stand against the Redskins had a lasting effect on all concerned.

Eli's Favorite Game

There would seem to be a predictable Eli Manning response to a seemingly-simple question: What is your favorite NFL game ever?

Super Bowl XLII would be the obvious choice. What else? Manning was the MVP of that epic 17-14 upset victory over the previously-undefeated Patriots, orchestrating the last-minute drive for the winning points and throwing the decisive touchdown pass with only 35 ticks remaining.

Yet Manning has a game he likes even better.

"Friends of mine who went to the Super Bowl and went to that game in Green Bay still talk about the Green Bay game more than the Super Bowl," Manning said.

"That game in Green Bay" was as good as any of those heralded, time-worn NFL battles of years gone by. NFL lore holds the "Ice Bowl" in high regard—an epic struggle in the 1967 NFL Championship Game, won by the Packers over the Cowboys, 21-17, on a frozen field in Green Bay. Forty years later, this was dubbed "Ice Bowl II," as the 2007 NFC Championship Game at historic Lambeau Field was the third-coldest game in league history—minus one degree on the thermometer, minus-23 wind chill on the field. Manning in his career had saved some of his worst games for the coldest weather. His legendary counterpart, Brett Favre, was truly the "Iceman," compiling a record of 43-5 at Lambeau when the temperature was below 34 degrees.

"My all-time favorite game," Manning recalls. "Not just because it was the NFC Championship Game. It was being in Green Bay, playing a game in negative 20 degrees. All those factors make a game special."

Manning, wearing a glove on his left hand but not on his right, thoroughly out-played Favre, completing 21 of 40 passes for 254 yards and three times put the Giants in position to seal the deal before Lawrence Tynes finally came through with a game-winning 47-yard field goal in overtime for a 23-20 Giants victory.

"It was beautiful," linebacker Antonio Pierce said. "Ice Bowl II with a different ending. A New York ending. Beautiful."

Overcoming the harsh conditions, Manning explained, "makes a game more special, they make it memorable. They make it memorable for players and for fans."

Manning made a believer out of even his most fervent critics, playing pitch-and-catch with receiver Plaxico Burress 11 times for 154 yards, often abusing Packers cornerback Al Harris, never turning the ball over with an interception. What will forever be etched in Giants legend is the way Manning sent Favre into retirement (briefly), the way Tynes recovered from his own failures not once but twice, and the way Tom Coughlin's cheeks turned beet-red, his players fearing for their head coach's health.

"I can't describe how bad it was," receiver Amani Toomer said of the cold. "Breathing in the air would burn your lungs, it was just ridiculous."

Kicking the frozen football was no fun, either. Immediately after the game, Tynes took off his shoe and sock to reveal a right foot that was completely black and blue, mostly black. The foot didn't return to normal color for eight days. It was 10 days before he was able to kick in preparation for the Super Bowl. Yet the Giants were almost sunk because of Tynes.

With 6:49 remaining in the fourth quarter and the game tied at 20, Tynes missed a 43-yard field goal attempt. Manning moved Tynes within range again, but on the final play of regulation, Tynes missed a 36-yard field goal attempt that would have ended the game right there, sending a knuckling kick wide right after a high snap from rookie Jay Alford.

After Favre was intercepted by cornerback Corey Webster—at the time it was thought to be the final pass of Favre's Hall of Fame career—the Giants had a shot at another field goal, but no one could have questioned Coughlin for feeling squeamish about sending Tynes back out there again. So Tynes took matters into his own hands (and feet), racing out onto the field before Coughlin ever called for the field goal unit. "I didn't want to give him any other chance to put me off the field," Tynes recalled.

The kick was true from 47 yards away and Tynes never stopped running, sprinting across the field and into the locker room as the Giants erupted in jubilation.

"That's kind of the Hallmark picture that was taken," Tynes said. "I never thought what the negative side of it would have been. It's obviously helped me stick around. I was fortunate Corey made a great play in overtime to get us the ball."

A classy Packers equipment manager retrieved the game-winning ball for Tynes, and it sits in his basement near a large picture of the winning kick. He's been offered plenty of money for the ball. "It's not for sale," Tynes says every time about a keepsake from Eli Manning's most favorite game.

The Rise and Fall of Plaxico

When the soft, crisp pass finally spiraled down from what seemed like the heavens for the Giants, Plaxico Burress thrust himself into franchise history, forever. It usually is only in childhood fantasies that a player hauls in the game-winning touchdown pass in the closing seconds to secure an improbable Super Bowl upset victory, but Burress turned fantasy into reality on a memorable night in Glendale, Arizona.

Playing in intense pain, having done next-to-nothing—one catch for 14 yards—in the first 59 minutes of Super Bowl XLII—Burress hooked up with Eli Manning for the decisive play with only 35 seconds remaining and the Giants trailing the heavily-favored Patriots 14-10. Burress, hobbled with a sprained left medial collateral ligament in his knee after slipping in the hotel shower a few days earlier and already playing with a chronic right ankle injury, ran a slant-and-go on cornerback Ellis Hobbs, pushed off his painful knee as Hobbs played the Giants receiver to cut inside. Instead, Burress cut outside, completely lost Hobbs, and was all alone in the left corner of the end zone to make the 13-yard reception that sent the Giants to a stunning 17-14 triumph, ending the Patriots bid for an undefeated 2007 season.

"This is the greatest feeling in professional sports," an emotional Burress exclaimed afterward. "It came down to one play and we made it."

HE made it.

"If anyone could ever know how close he came to not playing," Mike Sullivan, the Giants receivers coach at the time, marveled. "He shouldn't have been out there."

From that magic, exalted moment the fall was indeed precipitous for Burress. Nine months after a catch for the ages Burress was unknowingly sowing the final seeds of his Giants demise. A controversy-filled 2008 season turned disastrous when on a fateful early Saturday morning in late November he accidentally shot himself in the right thigh with an illegal handgun stuffed inside his sweatpants at a Manhattan nightclub. That shot ultimately became the death-knell for his Giants career, which officially ended in April of 2009 when the he was released by the team that ultimately could not deal with the towering, talented, but troubled receiver any longer.

How the mighty had fallen.

"This has been a tragic, sad, disappointing situation from the beginning," Giants spokesman Pat Hanlon said on September 23, 2009, the day Burress was sentenced to two years in prison for violating New York's stringent gun laws, the day he was taken into custody to begin a span of 20 months in jail.

Burress signed a free agent contract with the Giants in 2005 after flirting with his immense potential for five years with the Pittsburgh Steelers and instantly became the big-play receiver Manning needed. From the pinnacle of the game-winning catch in the Super Bowl, Burress descended into a personal and professional hell that left him unemployed and incarcerated. The demise came quickly—two days after his touchdown catch Burress didn't even attend the rousing tickertape victory parade through the Canyon of Heroes. He skipped out on a June minicamp because of a contract dispute before signing a five-year, $35-million deal just before the 2008 season opener.

Turmoil was his constant companion. He was suspended for 12 days, not allowed to play in a victory over the Seahawks because he missed team meetings, and then dodged calls from the team wondering about his whereabouts. "Plax is Plax, he does what he wants," teammate Steve Smith said when asked if Burress's absence from the wide receivers meeting attracted attention.

"We want to make sure that the message is loud and clear," head coach Tom Coughlin said of the suspension. "We've had success here because of the team concept. The team concept means that everyone is accountable and responsible, and we don't let the other guys down. We're trying to acknowledge that one of our guys has had a violation of team rules. We want him back, and we want him back under very good terms."

Burress did return, but against the 49ers in October he screamed at Coughlin after drawing an unsportsmanlike conduct penalty that prompted a $45,000 fine by the NFL for verbally abusing the officials. Coughlin benched Burress for the first quarter of a victory in Pittsburgh because he missed treatment on a neck and shoulder injury the day before the game. Burress admitted he lost count of all the fines he'd been hit with for violating team rules.

With the Giants rolling along at 10-1, Burress was sidelined with a hamstring injury that was going to keep him out of the next game in Washington. He went out on a Friday night the day after Thanksgiving with one of his teammates, linebacker Antonio Pierce, and it was at the Latin Quarter nightclub in Manhattan early the next morning where Burress accidentally shot himself with a .40-caliber gun he had concealed in his pants. He was treated and released from the hospital later Saturday afternoon, but not all wounds heal.

The Giants released Burress in April of 2009. New York City mayor Michael Bloomberg publicly called for Burress to be prosecuted to the fullest extent of the law. Burress eventually agreed to a plea deal, pleaded guilty to a lesser firearms charge, and was sent away, leaving behind his pregnant wife, Tiffany, and his almost three-year-old son, Elijah. Hours after Burress pleaded guilty, NFL commissioner Roger Goodell suspended Burress.

While imprisoned at Oneida Correctional Facility in upstate Rome, New York, Burress missed the birth of his daughter, Giovanna. He wrote a letter to the Giants owners, John Mara and Steve Tisch. "I told them how sorry I was about bringing all this bad publicity to such a stand-up organization," Burress said in a jailhouse interview, in which he also vowed, "I will play again." He was released from prison on June 6, 2011.

Moving Daze

Back in 2005, when a brand new home for the Giants was nothing more than an ambitious idea in the minds of some very wealthy men, a meeting was set to take place bringing together all parties interested in this very expensive project. John Mara, executive vice president of the Giants, asked his father Wellington—the patriarch of the New York Giants franchise—to attend the meeting.

Wellington Mara lived and breathed the Giants and NFL football, but he was not very interested in being present at this particular gathering. This was not all about football. Politicians would be there. So would shopping mall people and even Jets people, as the city's other New York franchise wanted to share the financial load for a new home. But Wellington Mara obliged the wishes of his oldest son and took a seat as the intricate and complex issues of building a mammoth new stadium were discussed.

Wellington Mara didn't last long at the meeting. He quickly excused himself.

"This is all too much for me," he said afterward, explaining his early departure. "I was happy in the Polo Grounds."

Time stands still for no one, and Wellington Mara's memories of the Polo Grounds—the first home of the football Giants, from 1925 to 1955—while vibrant were nonetheless resigned to history. The Polo Grounds gave way to Yankee Stadium and then to the Yale Bowl and then Shea Stadium (which they shared with the Jets) until 1976 with the opening of Giants Stadium, a lavish state-of-the-art facility outside the confines of New York, located amid the swamps of East Rutherford, New Jersey. Giants Stadium served the Giants well for 34 years—the Jets came aboard in 1984—and generations of Giants fans shared the agonies ("The Fumble" in 1978) and the ecstasies (two victorious NFC championship games) amid the swirling wind and great sightlines of the Giants Jersey home.

"When I think about Giants Stadium what comes to mind first are all the great games," John Mara said. "But, mostly it has been our home for a long time. It is where our offices have been, it's where my father's office was for many, many years. We had a lot of great moments and not so great moments there. It's been a major part of our lives for many, many years. Certainly, I can never forget that opening game and the excitement of that opening

game. Finally making the playoffs in 1981 by beating the Cowboys at the end of the season, in overtime. Obviously, the NFC
Championship Game in 1986 was a major moment for us. The
NFC Championship Game in 2000. There are certain games and
events that you never forget. I also remember the practices out on
the field, my father walking around the practice field, and a lot of
things like that will stay with me for years to come."

The lure of bigger and supposedly better ushered in the demise
of Giants Stadium, which was torn down following the 2009 season to make room for a parking lot adjacent to a state-of-the-art
monolith that cost $1.7 billion, making it the most expensive
sports stadium ever built. The only professional stadium shared by
two teams, the Giants and Jets had grand illusions of bidders paying tens of millions of dollars for naming rights, eager to pay for
the privilege of putting a corporate name on the new home of both
teams. The economic downturn, though, dashed that plan as bidders never materialized, and the rather generic "New Meadowlands
Stadium" was the fallback moniker.

Before settling into their new digs, the Giants were eager to
present Giants Stadium with a proper sendoff. Their 2009 season
was nothing to remember, but they were 8-6 and held slim hopes
of a playoff berth on December 27, 2009, when they played their
final game at Giants Stadium, against the underachieving Carolina
Panthers. This was an emotional day, kicked off with a video of
the top moments in the stadium's history. Once the game started,
the Giants added a disturbing stadium lowlight as they bid adieu
to their home in most unappealing fashion. They were devastated,
losing 41-9 in a game that they were embarrassed to offer up as the
curtain call in their old home.

"It's as low as I've been in a Giant uniform," defensive end
Justin Tuck said glumly. "The thing that's hard is they're showing

all those highlights and memories of LT [Lawrence Taylor] and [Phil] Simms and everybody that played here. And to have yourself be on a team that was booed off in the last game at Giants Stadium, I don't think you're going to get anybody that wants that to happen."

The Giants saved their worst for last, as Panthers running back Jonathan Stewart rushed for 206 yards—the most by a Giants opponent in Giants Stadium history.

"We disrespected this ground so much," running back Brandon Jacobs said, "that we don't deserve to play in the new spot."

Nine months later, the Giants did play in their new spot but not before some interesting infighting. The Giants and Jets both wanted the honor of opening the new stadium and were unable to settle the debate by themselves. NFL commissioner Roger Goodell stepped in by conducting a coin-flip in his office, with neither team present. He announced the Giants won the toss, giving them the stadium opener on September. 12, 2010. The next night, the Jets would get their shot on *Monday Night Football.*

Once again, it was the Panthers on the scene, just as they were the opponent to close out Giants Stadium, and this time the Giants held up their end, winning 31-18 in a New Meadowlands Stadium grand opening that was not always grand. It took the fans less than seven minutes in their sparkling new home to rain boos down on the home team after failing to pick up a first down on their first two offensive series.

"The fans are still the fans," reasoned defensive end Mathias Kiwanuka said.

Perhaps the fans were expressing a different form of frustration. Unlike the blue and red furnishings of Giants Stadium, the new place was basically all gray, a neutral palette in deference to two teams sharing one building, two inhabitants but neither truly homeowners. The waiting list for Giants season tickets for years was long and unmoving but the list was all-but pared down because of a huge rise in ticket prices—some as high as $700 per seat. In addition, attached to every seat was a Personal Seat License surcharge—as low as $1,000 per seat, as high as $20,000 per seat—for the right to keep seats in a family that in many cases were owned for decades.

The seating capacity at New Meadowlands Stadium was listed at 82,500, but the announced crowd for the stadium opener was 77,245, and the Giants admitted there were unsold seats, once an unheard of development.

"It's heartbreaking," running back Brandon Jacobs said after scanning the crowd, with some sections nearly devoid of fans.

The Giants call it progress, so many years after their patriarch was happy at the Polo Grounds.

Cut to the Chase

As the ball soared through the air, there was no reason to believe the Giants would win this matchup. No reason at all. After all, the combatants for Tom Brady's 50-yard toss were Rob Gronkowski, the dominating Patriots tight end, and Chase Blackburn, the nondescript Giants linebacker and career backup who not long before this decisive play in Super Bowl XLVI was out of football and contemplating life as a math teacher.

"It's unbelievable," Blackburn gushed after the play, and the game, went to the Giants. "Only God could draw this up. Nobody else could ever have imagined this."

Even those with the most fertile of imaginations would be hard-pressed to conjure up this tale. Blackburn went undrafted out of Akron and made his way onto the Giants' roster in 2005, earning a spot almost exclusively for his smarts and prowess on special teams. It was nice living, with Blackburn named the special teams captain three consecutive seasons. As a rookie on Christmas Eve, he made his first NFL start at linebacker against the Washington Redskins and took an interception of a Mark Brunell pass 31 yards for a touchdown.

Blackburn got a Super Bowl ring after the 2007 season, the prize for the Giants' upsetting the previously-unbeaten Patriots in Super Bowl XLII. He filled a role, found his niche, running downfield like a banshee on kickoff and punt coverage units, once in a while filling in at linebacker. When Antonio Pierce retired after the 2009 season, Blackburn did not get the call as the replacement at middle linebacker, as the Giants used Jonathan Goff, who they had drafted in 2008, to fill that assignment.

For six straight seasons, Blackburn led the Giants in special teams tackles, and an already-improbable career appeared destined for an ending, at the age of 28. Blackburn's contract had run out, the 2011 season arrived, and he was unsigned, which also means unwanted. Popularity among the coaching staff and among your teammates only goes so far.

"I bet you can ask anybody who was here, that was probably one of the biggest surprises, that Chase wasn't on the roster," linebacker and defensive end Mathias Kiwanuka said. "I mean, he was a special teams captain three years in a row. He comes early, he stays late, he's a good athlete, and he's always been prepared to make plays."

If this is where it ended, Blackburn figured he had a good run. He headed home to Dublin, Ohio, with his wife, Meagan, and two young sons. The Bengals, Rams, and Lions called and Blackburn dutifully traveled to work out for those teams. There were respectful "thanks but no thanks" partings, no contract offered.

Blackburn continued to work out back home, by himself. On Sundays, he would watch football, honing in most fervently on the

Giants, making the defensive calls audibly to no one but the television. From time to time, he would bark out the defensive signals to Meagan, watching alongside him.

By October, two months into the NFL season, Blackburn knew he had to at least consider making alternative plans. A former youth coach, a middle school principal, broached the idea of Blackburn becoming an eighth-grade math teacher, on a temporary basis, filling in as a substitute for a woman going on maternity leave. His life was starting to steer in a different direction, away from football.

The Giants, meanwhile, were a mess at linebacker. Clint Sintim was injured and lost for the season. The same with Goff, who tore up a knee. Rookie Greg Jones was given a shot at middle linebacker. Jacquian Williams, another rookie, got a look. So did Mark Herzlich, yet another rookie. Then Herzlich suffered a season-ending ankle injury on November 28, as the Giants were thrashed 49-24 in New Orleans, their third consecutive loss.

Something had to be done. General manager Jerry Reese knew it. He instructed Dave Gettleman, at the time the Giants' pro personnel director, to find someone.

"At the end of November, Jerry and I looked at each other and said 'We've got to bring Chase back,'" Gettleman said.

Kevin Abrams, the assistant general manager, made the call. Blackburn recognized the number on his phone as the Giants. Abrams asked Blackburn if he was in shape. Two hours later, Blackburn was on a flight to New Jersey.

"You know how people talk about 'Oh, he's in the right place at the right time?'" linebacker Michael Boley said. "That's not because they're lucky. It's because they planned to be there. It's a talent."

The return was met with widespread joy inside the Giants locker room.

"You would've thought Ray Nitschke, Sam Huff, and Dick Butkus had walked in," Gettleman said. "The respect the players had for him was huge."

There was no fear Blackburn would be blindsided by the defensive playbook; defensive coordinator Perry Fewell often marveled that Blackburn knew it better than he did. Still, the prevailing sentiment was the Giants signed Blackburn off the couch and, less than a week later, he would be their starting middle linebacker against Aaron Rodgers and the Packers.

In his first game in nearly one calendar year, Blackburn intercepted a Rodgers pass in the second quarter—one of only six interceptions thrown by Rodgers in 502 attempts that season. The Giants lost 38-35.

"Sometimes you just need that opportunity," Boley said. "That is all it is. You get your shot and you make the most of it."

The Giants, with their improbable defensive signal-caller directing traffic, went on an improbable run. With Blackburn calling the shots as the starter, the Giants went 6-1. In the NFC divisional playoff game in Green Bay, Blackburn scooped up a fumble and raced 40 yards to the Packers' four-yard line, finally run down by Rodgers.

All this was precursor to that ball thrown by Tom Brady on the second play of the fourth quarter in Super Bowl XLVI, with the Giants trailing 17-15. The ball hung in the air inside Lucas Oil Stadium in Indianapolis, where Blackburn and Gronkowski were set to battle for it at the Giants' eight-yard line. Gronkowski was dealing with a sprained ankle and Brady was under some pressure before uncoiling his throw. Still, Blackburn's strength as a player was never deemed to be his deep coverage ability or finding himself 50 yards from the line of scrimmage; this was far away from his comfort zone. Plus, Gronkowski is a beast.

Gronkowski initially had Blackburn beat, but Blackburn was able to recover, set himself, and leapt for the ball. He came down with it, the first turnover of the game for either team.

"It was like going up for a rebound in basketball," Blackburn said. "I was able to get in great position."

The Patriots were thwarted, and the Giants went on to a rousing 21-17 victory, earning a second championship ring for Blackburn, who had six tackles in the game in addition to an interception that will forever be a part of Giants lore.

Blackburn started 15 games for the Giants in 2012. They offered their 29-year-old overachiever a one-year contract to stay, but the Panthers—with Gettleman, one of Blackburn's biggest fans, moved on as the general manager in Carolina, offering him two. Blackburn's eight years with the Giants had come to an end.

Blackburn took to Twitter to bid adieu: "Thanks for 8 great years Giants. But it's time for the next chapter."

Super Mario

The magic and microphones of NFL Films captured it, moments before Mario Manningham caught it.

Here the Giants were again, trying to catch the Patriots late in a Super Bowl, backed up on the 12-yard line with 3:46 remaining, trailing 17-15, needing a spark, a burst of energy, a chunk of yards, and, eventually, needing the points required to pull off an upset. It was almost the same situation they were in four years earlier, when Eli Manning threw it and a largely unknown receiver named David Tyree caught it, off his helmet, no less, for the seminal play in one of the most significant upsets in NFL history.

This time, in Super Bowl XLVI, everyone knew Manning was going to throw it. He had dangerous targets in Hakeem Nicks and

Victor Cruz. Bill Belichick, the Patriots' all-knowing head coach, knew this. And, before sending his defense out on the field for a final stand, Belichick—one of the greatest defensive masterminds to ever work in the league—once again went over the game plan to his players, leaving no doubt as to his wishes.

"This is still a Cruz and Nicks game," Belichick barked into his headset, in audio captured by NFL Films. "I mean, I know we're right on 'em, it's tight. But those are still the guys. Make 'em go to Manningham, make 'em go to Pascoe, all right? But let's make sure we get Cruz and Nicks."

Nothing genius here—this was the obvious defensive thrust for the Patriots. Manningham was the Giants' No. 3 receiver. Bear Pascoe was a blocking tight end with limited pass-catching skills. Do not let the big guys beat you. Make Manning throw it to players posing less-present danger.

What Belichick feared is what Manning and the Giants desired. Manning wanted to go to the right, where both Nick and Cruz lined up, but the Patriots were there, waiting, as their head coach instructed.

"They were in cover-2," Manning said. "Usually that is not your matchup. They had us covered pretty well to the right. I looked that way."

Manning did not like what he saw. He noticed a blitz brewing on the left side and adjusted his call, alerting Pascoe to stay in and counter the blitz with a blocking assignment. Manning also noticed the Patriots' safeties dropping deep. Manningham, lined up on the left side, had been coached to run a "go" route against this coverage.

Nicks and Cruz to the right ran corner routes. They were well-covered, and Manning did not have much time to wait for them to spring open, as nose tackle Vince Wilfork tried to power through guard Kevin Boothe, collapsing the pocket and threatening to invade Manning's territory.

There was not much time, but Manning had the poise to look to the right, even though he already knew he could not throw the ball that way. Manning's glance was a ruse and it ensnared safety Patrick Chung, who turned his hips ever so slightly, a slight adjustment in case the pass went to the other side of the field.

Manningham, a shifty receiver blessed with superior elusiveness, ran by cornerback Sterling Moore and raced up the left sideline. Chung, supposed to provide help over the top, was a step late with his help. Manning, backed up on his 5-yard line, uncorked the throw despite Wilfork's hand in his face. The pass, a high, precise floater angled to the left side, looked as if it would drift out of bounds. It was not a high-percentage attempt against this particular defense, at this particular time.

"I saw the safety cheated a little bit and threw it down the sideline," Manning said.

"Most quarterbacks would be scared to throw that," added Manningham.

At first, it appeared Manningham had little chance to make the catch. First, he was all but tiptoeing the sideline—there was precious little room. Second, with the ball in the air, Moore caught up to Manningham and chopped down on the right shoulder of the receiver. The time it took for the ball to land also gave Chung a second chance and he was on the scene as well.

The only recourse for Manningham was to attempt a difficult over-the-shoulder catch with two defenders bearing down on him and the sideline pressing up against him. Manningham said he knew he had to "freeze my feet when the ball touched my fingertips. I knew I was going to either get hit or hit the ground. I knew something was going to happen.

"But I knew I couldn't let that ball go."

Later, reflecting back, Manningham said, "Good thing I wear size 11. I don't think I'd have been in with an 11 1/2."

The catch was made as Manningham and the defenders tumbled out of bounds. The Giants were on the 50-yard line with 3:39 remaining. Incredulous, desperate, or both, Belichick called for a replay, challenging that the catch was made in-bounds.

"It was close," Belichick said. "Real close."

As replays were shown on the monitors inside Lucas Oil Stadium, Giants fans cheered what they believed they saw. Watching intently down on the field, Cruz studied the entirety of the play. "Catch right, left, yes!" he exclaimed.

Moments later, Belichick and the Patriots received the bad news. Good catch, gain of 38 for the Giants.

"It was a big, big, big-time play right there," Manning said.

It might have been the most accurate throw of Manning's career.

"That was a phenomenal throw and catch," a grudgingly admiring Tom Brady said.

"Eli put a perfect pass in there," said Moore in what was a crushing end to his rookie season. "There wasn't much room to get in there. Hat's off to Eli for making that pass. But I've got to get more on [Manningham] at the line to give Patrick a chance to get over there. That's on me."

Manningham caught two more passes in the nine-play, 88-yard drive, with Ahmad Bradshaw scoring the decisive touchdown in a 21-17 Giants victory, the second time in four years a Manning pass fell from the sky and smote the Patriots. Four years after David Tyree, there was Mario Manningham.

"They're both spectacular catches," Giants coach Tom Coughlin said. "I think with Mario's, the way he kept his feet in bounds and held on to the ball without going out of bounds, it was a remarkable thing.

"Of course, David's is forever and that's the history. That's never going to change anything. His was incredible. This just continues along that fashion."

The Catch

In the official NFL game book, this is the first line that appears in the scoring summary for the second quarter of the November 23, 2014, NFC East clash between the Giants and Cowboys at MetLife Stadium:

14:52: O. Beckham 43 pass from E. Manning (J. Brown kick) (6-66, 2:53).

That is it, one line describing one touchdown throw and catch, the extra point, and duration and time of the scoring drive. If three more words were added, it would be these: Life-altering moment.

"It's kind of one of those things—it's changed my life forever, and not in a bad way," Odell Beckham Jr. explained.

Those who were there in person, the paying customers, could not believe what they saw in real time, and then again, slowed down, on the video screen. On the field, Beckham's teammates were in awe and the Cowboys were in shock. Those who were watching on television, after repeated high-definition replays provided freeze-frame evidence, were incredulous, and too many of them to count took to social media, needing to express themselves in a shared, wide-eyed communal disbelief.

"There's your play of the year and maybe, I don't know, the decade," exclaimed play-by-play announcer Al Michaels to the viewers on NBC for the *Sunday Night Football* national telecast. "That's just incredible."

Beckham, a heralded 22-year-old rookie selected by the Giants out of LSU with the 12th overall pick in the 2014 NFL Draft, endured a sluggish yet promising start to his NFL career. He missed the first four games dealing with a hamstring injury, caught a touchdown pass in his first NFL game, and caught two more against the Cowboys in his third game, in Arlington, Texas. He notched his first 100-yard receiving game in a loss at Indianapolis.

Nothing, though, prepared him for the injection of fame he experienced in the Week 12 rematch with the Cowboys in East Rutherford, New Jersey. The Giants led 7-3 when Eli Manning, on the first play of the second quarter, looked deep down the right sideline, where Beckham was double-covered, with cornerback Brandon Carr running with the young receiver and safety Barry Church lurking to prevent anything over the top. Carr and Beckham jostled for position along the right sideline, with Carr pinning down Beckham's left arm. Beckham kept his legs churning, freed his left arm, and glided past Carr, who again made contact with the ball in the air. John Jenkins, the field judge, tossed a yellow penalty flag for pass interference on Carr.

Manning's lofted pass seemed destined to carry out of bounds. Beckham, having finally escaped from Carr's clutches, leaped while falling backward. Only his right arm reached up into the sky and only three fingers on his big right hand made contact with the ball. Somehow, the ball stuck, and Beckham was able to secure it with only his right hand, perilously close to landing out of bounds as he crashed, backside first, into the right corner of the end zone, just inside the pylon. Officially, it was a 43-yard touchdown. Spiritually, it was the arrival of a megastar.

On the telecast, analyst Cris Collinsworth, a former NFL receiver, said, "That is absolutely impossible what he just did."

Down on the field, the Cowboys' disappointment at allowing a touchdown gave way to incredulity upon seeing the replay. "At first

I was like, 'OK, he had a great catch, whatever,'" Church said. "But when I saw it on the big screen it was just ridiculous."

Up in the luxury suites, Stephen Jones, the Cowboys' executive vice president, at first thought the ball would soar over Beckham's reach.

"Somebody said 'He caught that ball,'" Jones said. "I said 'What?' I couldn't believe it. I looked at the board. It has to be the best catch I've ever seen."

Giants receiver Victor Cruz, injured and watching from a suite, instantly knew he had seen greatness.

"I've been around football my whole life and been a part of a lot of great games and been a part of a lot of great catches myself," he said, "so I've seen a lot, but that catch was by far the best one I've seen."

It took no time at all for social media to erupt.

Seahawks cornerback Richard Sherman took to Twitter to exclaim "My Goodness . . . that young man is bad!!!" Hall of Fame receiver Andre Reed tipped his cap on Twitter, writing "Made some crazy catches in my day but 13 for the G – Men just trumped them all . . . #Crazycatch."

Another receiver, Randy Moss, a future Hall of Famer, was asked about Beckham's catch.

"I don't have one that compares to that at all in my career," Moss said.

The catch heard 'round the world could not be contained. NBA superstar LeBron James was duly impressed. Moments after the catch, he tweeted "Man I just witnessed the greatest catch ever possibly by Odell Beckham Jr! WOW!!!!"

At halftime, Odell Beckham Jr. was trending on Twitter.

Tom Coughlin, the hard-to-impress Giants head coach, knew what he had seen was uncommon.

"He's got a gift, there's no doubt," Coughlin said. "I've seen him make a lot of one-handed catches, to be honest with you. But none falling down like that, going away and being able to snatch the ball like that and then stay in bounds after being fouled. That was quite a thing, too."

The Giants ended up losing the game, 31-28. Despite playing in only 12 games, Beckham had the greatest rookie season in NFL history with 91 receptions for 1,305 yards and 12 touchdowns. He became the first Giants player to be named the league's Offensive Rookie of the Year in the 59-year history of the award.

It was one of the 91 rookie receptions that turned Beckham into a celebrity.

Beckham, astonished by the outpouring of attention and acclaim, acknowledged it was probably the greatest catch he'd ever made in a game. "I hope it's not the greatest catch of all time," he said. "I hope I can make more."

Reflecting back on the catch after his first season, Beckham said, "There were so many other things I did during the season. It's hard for me to distinguish myself because of that catch. I know that I'm more than that. But at least people know you, you know what I mean?"

"It's Not Your Fault."

This was the last time he would be referred to as Tom Coughlin, head coach of the New York Giants, and 12 years of achievement, emotion, grand success, and, yes, abject failure all flowed out of this most extraordinary press conference.

Officially, Coughlin was stepping down, stepping aside, set to cede the coveted position of head coach of the Giants. This was the way ownership and upper management wanted this parting to go, Coughlin leaving on his own terms, a respectful farewell for such a noble gentleman. Coughlin earned two more Lombardi

Trophies for the glass-enclosed case inside the team's practice facility, a coach who presented the franchise with two of the most unlikely Super Bowl triumphs in NFL history.

Unofficially, if Coughlin had put up a fight, citing the one year remaining on his contract, daring Giants ownership to fire him, it would not have gone well for him, and he knew it. So, on Monday, January 4, 2016, one day after ending the 2015 campaign with a 35-30 loss to the Eagles to, mercifully, close the curtain on a season that ended with a record of a 6-10, Coughlin met with the Giants' top brass and fell on his sword. "I informed them that it is in the best interest of the organization that I step down as head coach," was the wording in the statement he issued that day.

This cold and programmed goodbye would not suffice, and a day later, Coughlin, as he had done so many times in the past dozen years, stood behind a lectern at the team facility intent on delivering a message. This time, rather than addressing a room full of his players and coaches, there was only a handful of players on hand, seated up near the front, with members of the media, photographers, and television cameras filling the space.

Coughlin, always fully in charge in these surroundings, admitted he had never been as nervous to stand up and speak. He noted it was an honor to coach the Giants—"It's something you only dream about as a kid"—and reminisced about watching, on his black-and-white TV while growing up in a modest home in Waterloo in upstate New York, the fabled Giants teams on the small screen.

Coughlin ran down a list of members of the organization to thank, leaving out no one, and flinched only when mentioning his wife, Judy, which forced Coughlin to choke back emotion.

It was when Coughlin spotted Eli Manning, his quarterback for every one of those 12 years, biting his lip, his face quivering as he fought back tears, that the grizzled 69-year-old coach let down his guard, fully and completely.

A day earlier, Manning stood at his locker and addressed what everyone knew was impending, saying it was his fault, and the fault of his teammates, that Coughlin was getting forced out.

Since the stunning victory in Super Bowl XLVI, the Giants had gone four consecutive years without making the playoffs. Their records of 9-7, 7-9, 6-10, and 6-10 represented regression; the arrow was not pointing up. Coughlin's final years were unkind, with the Giants leading the league in injuries three years running. The 2015 season was quietly, but forcefully, designated as one last chance for Coughlin to make it right. But Coughlin had no chance, not with general manager Jerry Reese unable to supply enough talent to fortify a shabby defense. The Giants in 2015 averaged more than 26 points a game, robust production that should have spawned playoff contention, at the very least. But their defense was bad, historically so, allowing 422 points, and Coughlin was so spooked by giving up lead after lead late in games that he frequently went against his better judgment, making decisions based on the legitimate fear his defense could not hold up, at all, ever.

Such was the case in a December 6 game against the Jets, with Coughlin's clock management and in-game decision-making once again called into question. The Giants were ahead 20-10 early in the fourth quarter, poised to kick a routine field goal to extend their lead to 13 points. Coughlin, putting no trust in the ability of his defense to protect a 13-point lead, eschewed the kick, went for it on fourth down, and Manning's pass was intercepted. Sure enough, Coughlin's trepidation about his defense was well-founded, and the Giants lost 23-20 in overtime.

Desperate is no way to coach, but Coughlin, saddled with such a terrible defense, was coaching desperate. When questioned and ridiculed for his decision, Coughlin shot back thusly: "To be honest with you, nobody knows my team better than I know my team."

A month later, Coughlin was standing behind that lectern, saying goodbye, knowing Manning had put the blame on himself, seeing his quarterback ready to break down. The question was asked: What would Coughlin's message be to Manning, who had never played for any other head coach in the NFL?

"He can handle it all," Coughlin said. "He's done it before. He can handle it again. He's extremely bright. He's extremely competitive. He's what you want a son to be made out of."

That last line got to Manning, who appeared ready to lose it. Coughlin, perhaps for the final time, tried to shepherd his quarterback to safety.

Coughlin pointed to Manning.

"He thinks he's the reason," Coughlin said, his voice rising. "He's not the reason. Eli, it's not you. It's not you. It's us. We win, we lose together. When we lose, I lose. When we win, you guys win. That's the way it is. That's the game. I know what it is. I got the game. I got it.

"But what I would tell him, he's going to be right here in about two days starting to work on next year, just like he always does. That's never going to change. God bless him for it."

Coughlin in 12 years guided the Giants to 102 regular-season victories—only Steve Owen (153) had more. Coughlin's eight postseason victories as head coach of the Giants matched Bill Parcells for most in team history. Coughlin left the Giants as one of thirteen NFL coaches to win multiple Super Bowls.

"It is difficult to come up with words adequate to describe the appreciation we have for everything Tom Coughlin has done for our franchise," co-owner John Mara said.

McAdoo Suits the Giants

If clothes make the man, Ben McAdoo was destined for an extra-large impact with the Giants.

McAdoo was introduced as the 17th head coach of the New York Giants on January 15, 2016. At 38, he was the second-youngest coach in the NFL, and he replaced Tom Coughlin, who at 69 had been the league's oldest coach. For members of Giants' ownership and the front office, the players, the media that covered the team, and fans who cheered for the Giants, there was a sense of familiarity to this hire, as McAdoo was Coughlin's offensive coordinator the previous two seasons.

Everyone in the building knew McAdoo. Or, they all thought they knew McAdoo—until he showed up for his first press conference as head coach.

McAdoo wore a suit that was, to be kind, rather large on him.

"You could say I'm more comfortable in sweats and a hoodie," McAdoo said. "I like to grind, I like to work. It's always good to have something you can grind in. But you have to be presentable as well."

The oversized suit, McAdoo explained, was a relic from his past, when he was about sixty pounds heavier. In the whirlwind that swept him up as the 2015 season came to an end and a few weeks later he was chosen to replace Coughlin, McAdoo did not have time to shop for new attire. He joked the weight he lost was akin to "a third grader."

So, how did he think he looked in his old, baggy suit?

"Like a third grader," he said, smiling.

As per usual, social media had a field day with McAdoo's "roomy" suit. Fashion experts chimed in, offering suggestions. It was not the most auspicious debut for a small-town guy from Homer City, Pennsylvania, designated as the replacement for one of the most storied coaches in Giants franchise history.

"I can't worry about being in Tom's shadow," McAdoo said. "I have to be comfortable in my own skin."

McAdoo paid homage to Coughlin, insisting that the clocks at the team facility remain five minutes fast, known as "Coughlin time"—Coughlin's way of instilling an "on time is late" mentality during his 12 years running the show and setting the schedule.

"We're going to stick with that," McAdoo said. "That's TC time. That's part of Giants culture now."

Part of Giants culture the last four years of Coughlin's watch was watching the playoffs from home. Upon taking the job, McAdoo was unafraid to set as a goal the prize Coughlin twice delivered to the franchise.

"This job is not for the faint of heart, and I'm the right man for the job," McAdoo said. "I'm hardened, battle-tested, and I've been groomed for this opportunity by Super Bowl-winning coaches, players, and organizations."

Prior to coming to the Giants in 2014, McAdoo spent eight years in Green Bay as an assistant coach for Mike McCarthy.

"The vision for this football team goes into winning and putting that fifth Lombardi Trophy in the case," McAdoo said. "That is our goal and that is our vision."

McAdoo described his vision for returning the Giants to prominence as "evolution, not revolution." He said, "We're not looking to rebuild. We're looking to reload."

McAdoo's roster in his first year as a head coach was fortified with an influx of talent on defense—a necessary ingredient Coughlin was not afforded in his final two seasons. General manager Jerry Reese spent nearly $200 million to sign defensive end Olivier Vernon, cornerback Janoris "Jackrabbit" Jenkins, and defensive tackle Damon "Snacks" Harrison, instantly upgrading what was a terrible 2015 unit. The offense McAdoo as coordinator prodded so much production out of often fell flat in 2016 with him as head coach—he also called the offensive plays—but a series of strong defensive showings steered the Giants to a record of 11-5 and a return to the playoffs for the first time in four years.

"Giants fans everywhere, I realize that this fan base is tough, it's passionate, and deserves a winner," McAdoo said. "This is the capital of the world, and this is the football capital of the world. And with that comes a certain amount of pressure, a pressure I look forward to."